"Stephen McAlpine has written a book that we desperately need. It's searching, sane, deeply biblical and, best of all, profoundly encouraging. If you want to understand what's going on in our world right now, then you need to read this book. If you want to work out what it means to live faithfully at school, at university, at work and even at home, then you need to read this book. If you have ever felt like the 'bad guy', then you really do need to read this book. Perhaps I haven't been clear enough: I think everyone needs to read this book!"

Gary Millar, Principal, Queensland Theological College, Australia

"With piercing insight, McAlpine skilfully draws parallels between the battles we face today in our culture and familiar Bible stories, impelling us to stand up courageously for the truth of the gospel against a tide of opposition. Through this book I have been forewarned and forearmed by the gospel, which he applies in a clear, radical, inspiring and relevant way. A timely wake-up call that has already proved invaluable in my personal witness."

Linda Allcock, Author, *Deeper Still*

"As an Asian kid growing up in the West, I was never sure if my loyalty was to the Hong Kong we left behind or the Australia we now found ourselves in. This is also what it's like to be a Christian in our new 21st-century society. Do we long for a Christendom that is no longer there? Or do we set up camp in this post-Christendom world? But what does that even look like? In *Being the Bad Guys*, Stephen McAlpine equips Christians to live in the new norm—a world that sees Christians as the bad guys. This is both a wake-up call and the toolkit that we need to survive and thrive. Now, just as in the times of Daniel in Babylon, is the time for us to shine."

Sam Chan, City Bible Forum, Australia;
Author, *Evangelism in a Skeptical World*

"Stephen McAlpine doesn't just describe the chilling change in our Western cultural climate. He also shows the way to follow Jesus through the storms."

Collin Hansen, Editorial Director, The Gospel Coalition

"If the men of Issachar 'understood the times and knew what to do' (1 Chronicles 12 v 32), then Stephen McAlpine has written an Issacharine book! With deft cultural analysis and profoundly biblical lenses, he helps us see the shape of faithful Christian living in our age. And while our challenges feel new, McAlpine insists that they find deep, challenging and illuminating parallels in the history of God's people. With the help of Abraham, Daniel, Haggai and the Corinthians, McAlpine points us to cross-shaped, Christ-like, Spirit-filled wisdom that will bless and fortify a new generation—inspiring them to follow Jesus."

Glen Scrivener, Evangelist; Author, *Long Story Short*

"McAlpine is neither superficial nor simplistic. He recognises the complexity of the spaghetti-like strands of the culture in which we live. However, rather than paralysis or retreat, he offers Christians and their church communities biblically wise and practical yet strategic suggestions. Recommended."

Dan Strange, Director, Oak Hill College, London; Author, *Plugged In*

"This is a must-read for anyone grappling to understand the staggering changes in our society as all the old certainties—and notions of how we relate to each other—are suddenly swept out to sea and replaced by a strident new authoritism that seeks to drown out all dissent. McAlpine is deeply perceptive and writes with the simple clarity that only a master of complex issues can provide. At last we can find a neat and accessible explanation of what is happening in our culture."

John Anderson, Former Deputy Prime Minister of Australia

"It's undoubtedly a fallacy to think that any period of history has been static, free from any significant societal change. But it's undoubtedly equally true that in our particular period of history we are witnessing change that is both swift and seismic. One of the most jarring changes for Christians has been our transformation from being good guys to bad guys. At a time like this we need guidance on how to live for Jesus, and that's exactly the guidance Stephen McAlpine so aptly provides in this excellent book."

Tim Challies, Blogger; Author, *Epic* and *Visual Theology*

"For too many Christians, the biggest fear is that they will be out of step with the culture; but Jesus promises that to follow him is to be, at some points, at odds with the ethos of a fallen world. Pastor Stephen McAlpine offers a refreshing call to Christian courage—and yet urges Christians to avoid rudeness and incivility. Readers will come away with both a newfound boldness to live for Christ in a confusing world and a countercultural joy that will radiate in their public and private witness."

Daniel Darling, Senior Vice-President of Communications, NRB; Author, *A Way with Words* and *The Dignity Revolution*

"There are books that tell us about the culture, there are books that tell us about evangelism, there are books that tell us about apologetics, there are books that tell us about the local church—but what I love about *Being the Bad Guys* is that it does all four. Stephen McAlpine is an astute cultural observer, an experienced pastor and an excellent writer. I hope that this will be read widely not only by church leaders but by any Christian who wants to understand where we are and where we should be."

David Robertson, Director, Third Space, Sydney

"Clear, contemporary and compelling. This is an outstanding book which lays out in a highly accessible way the main contours of how our present society is hostile to Christianity, and how Christians and the church could respond in a biblical, God-honouring, soul-winning way."

Melvin Tinker, Former Vicar of St John's Newland, Hull, UK

"This is the most sensible book I've read in a long time! By which I mean, Stephen explains with clarity and realism how modern culture no longer sees Christian belief as quaint but views it with suspicion or worse. Yet this is no counsel of despair. Rather, it offers a truthful and faithful path forward which will give Christians confidence and grit as they hold out the word of life to a highly confused world."

Matt Fuller, Author, *Be True to Yourself*

Being the Bad Guys

How to Live for Jesus in a World That Says You Shouldn't

Stephen McAlpine

thegoodbook
COMPANY

To Jill, who has helped me live for Jesus

Being the Bad Guys
© Stephen McAlpine, 2021. Reprinted 2021.

Published by:
The Good Book Company

thegoodbook.com | thegoodbook.co.uk
thegoodbook.com.au | thegoodbook.co.nz | thegoodbook.co.in

ISBN: 9781784985981 | Printed in the UK

Cover design by Spencer Fuller, Faceout Studio | Art direction by André Parker

Contents

Introduction 9

Part One: *How Did We Get to Be the Bad Guys?*

1. Why This Sudden Hostility? 15

2. Why the Surprise? 31

Part Two: *What Being the Bad Guys Looks Like*

3. Binary Beige Versus Diverse Rainbows 45

4. Loud Power Versus Voiceless Victims 61

5. Self-Denial Versus Self-Actualisation 77

Part Three: *Being the Best Bad Guy You Can Be*

6. Don't Renovate the Wrong House
   (A Strategy for Church) 93

7. When the War Comes to You
   (A Strategy for the Workplace) 109

8. The City and the City 125

Afterword 141

Acknowledgements 143

Introduction

"**Y**ou mean *I'm* the bad guy? How did that happen?"
It's not easy to be the baddie. It's particularly disconcerting when you didn't use to be, but then you suddenly realise that that's how others see you. And so it is that this line, from the 1993 film *Falling Down*, has lodged itself in the front of my mind in the last couple of years. It stars Michael Douglas as William Foster, who starts his day (and the film) as an average law-abiding guy. He ends it as the bad guy on the wrong side of the law—and it comes as a complete surprise to him. He has no idea how it has happened or how to deal with it.

Most Christians don't have much in common with Douglas's character, William Foster. I don't know you personally, but I'm guessing that, unlike Foster, you haven't threatened anyone with a rocket launcher or shot a police officer. But I am guessing that in the past year or so you've had a conversation with a non-Christian neighbour that didn't go well, or you've overheard a discussion between work colleagues expressing anger over Christian views on a particular issue, or you've read or watched a piece in the media taking potshots at biblical ethics. And you've thought to yourself something like:

"You mean we're the bad guys? How, when, why did that happen?"

Because, yes, in the eyes of much of Western society, Christianity is the bad guy (or at least is fast becoming so). Christianity is the problem. And it's happened so quickly that it's taken us by surprise.

Only a few generations ago, Christianity was the good guy, the solution to what was bad. Rather than being on the wrong side of the law, we were the law. Christian morality was assumed and passed mainly unchallenged. The cultural, legal and political power structures affirmed Christians. Then something changed. Over the course of the twentieth century, we became just one of the guys: one option among many—a voice to be considered but not to be followed unquestioningly. If Christianity worked for you, fine; if it didn't work for me, also fine.

Most of us think we still live in that world. Most Christian books, sermons and podcasts assume that we do. In many ways, we've only just worked out how to live well as one of the guys.

But the problem is that that's not where we are now. The tide has shifted further. Increasingly Christianity is viewed as the bad guy. Christianity is no longer an option; it's a problem. The cultural, political and legal guns that

Christianity once held are now trained on us—and it's happened quickly. The number of those professing faith has fallen dramatically. The number of those who reject the faith they held until their late teens has risen dramatically. The seat at the cultural table that we assumed was ours for keeps is increasingly being given to others. We're on the wrong side of history, the wrong side of so many issues and conversations. If this were a Western, we would be the guys wearing the black hats whose appearance is accompanied by the foreboding soundtrack. It's come as a surprise, we're not sure how it happened, we don't like it and we don't feel like we deserve it—but we are the bad guys now.

So what do we do about it?

The Best Bad Guy

Being on the wrong side is tiring and demoralising. It makes us feel defeated or angry. But I'm not going to tell you how to stop being one of the bad guys, because the only way to stop being a bad guy in the eyes of the world is to become what the world says is a good guy. And right now, that means compromising in all kinds of areas where the world beckons one way and the Bible points another. So this book isn't about how to stop being the bad guys; it's about how to be the bad guys. It's about how to be the best bad guy you can be—to refuse to be surprised, confused, despairing and mad about it, and to find a way to be calm, clear-sighted, confident and even joyful in it.

After all, this isn't new. If we look back far enough, we'll see that God's people have been "the bad guys" before. Scripture assumes it. Jesus predicted it. The apostles experienced it. The church, in most times and in most places, has lived it. Now the baton passes to us.

Before we start, two things are worth mentioning. First, Western culture is not always wrong. When secular society calls out Christians as bad guys, our first question should be: are they right? We have to acknowledge that the church has a mixed history, and when the church enjoyed power and influence, too often it used it in exactly the opposite way to its founder: to serve itself, to make its members comfortable. We have often been too little like Jesus, and for that we need to stop trying to justify or excuse ourselves, and hold our hands up, apologise, and do better. We have been perpetrators who made life hard for others who we decided were "bad guys". Not every critical voice is simply out to get us, and some critical voices have much to teach us; there are genuine wrongs that we need to right. Yet at the same time, the fact is that often we are accused of doing wrong not because we are living too little like Jesus but because we are living too much like him.

Which brings me to the second thing. In this book, a lot of the time we'll be thinking about the way Western secularism and biblical Christianity have diametrically opposed views on many areas of sexual ethics and gender identity. That's because 21st-century Western culture sees accepting its take on these things as fundamental to human identity, freedom, and flourishing—and so it is the territory in which Christians are most of all seen as the bad guys, where biblical ethics are not seen merely as laughable or outdated or repressed but as shameful, harmful and repressive. Our views are not merely seen as wrong but dangerous. Christians are sometimes accused of being obsessed about sex, and I suppose this book would seem to give credence to that charge. But the reason we talk about it, and the reason this book will keep returning to it, is because our culture talks so much about it and brooks no compromise over it. Increasingly, the first question we're asked when people realise we are Bible-believing Christians is not "Do you believe dinosaurs existed?" (a question often asked back when I was young) but "What do you think about homosexuality?" or "Where do you stand on same-sex marriage?" The charge is that not to believe in dinosaurs is stupid, but not to agree with same-sex marriage is bad.

Yes, we're the bad guys now. And that's ok. That we are experiencing a backlash after a remarkable period of religious peace and tolerance for the church in the West puts us back in the shoes of many Christians throughout history, and indeed of many in the current era around the world. The answers to how to live as bad guys are there, simply because the problem of finding ourselves rejected by the world has always been there. As we explore the problem and then unpack the answers the Bible offers, we will find ourselves able to do what many Christians have done down the ages: live holy, happy, loving and joyous lives that compel as many people as they repel: to be the best bad guys we can be.

1. Why This Sudden Hostility?

British doctor David Mackereth lost his job in 2019 for saying he would not use preferred pronouns for transgender patients, on the basis of his Christian beliefs about gender and sexuality. He took his employer to a tribunal hearing. He lost his case.

That was a shock to Dr Mackereth, but it is the reason the court gave for its findings that is most revealing. It was Dr Mackereth's use of Genesis 1 v 27 and its binary view of male and female that proved to be his downfall. His religious conviction did not protect his position; instead the tribunal stated:

"Belief in Genesis 1:27, lack of belief in transgenderism and conscientious objection to transgenderism in our judgment are incompatible with human dignity and conflict with the fundamental rights of others, specifically here, transgender individuals."[1]

The catchcry of "equal value, dignity and worth" is grounded upon the biblical statement that humans are made in the image of God. For the Christian, this reality is enhanced by the incarnation, in which God became a man—one of us. Historian Tom Holland observes that these convictions did not arise from the ether. They are not "fundamental":

"That human beings have rights; that they are born equal; that they are owed sustenance and shelter, and refuge from persecution: these were never self evident truths."[2]

Holland explains that the "universal" human-rights declarations of organisations such as the United Nations are in fact quite local and historical, finding their origins in documents drawn up by canon lawyers in medieval Europe. That is, they have not always and everywhere been accepted or even thought of. They spring from the truths of Genesis 1. Yet in one pronouncement by Dr Mackereth's judge, his belief in those truths was not merely dismissed as archaic but denounced as dangerous.

And that is but one example. Every day my social-media feeds are clogged with headlines from Christian organisations railing against yet another political action or legal judgment against Christian practices and values.

Christians feel shock as new laws are passed across the Western world which preference LGBTQI rights over religious freedoms. There is anger over unsuccessful challenges to late-term abortion and euthanasia laws. There is worry that efforts to keep Scripture in schools will fail, or that moves to cut funding for religious charities will succeed. And all this against a backdrop of global persecution against Christians which gets little to no oxygen in the mainstream media.

The question we may ask is not simply, "How did this happen?" but "How did this happen so quickly?" Wasn't it only yesterday that Christianity was begrudgingly accepted as a societal good? A bit like taking cod-liver oil in the fifties: not all that palatable, but beneficial. But now? It's not only unpalatable; it's positively toxic—and now it's time to get rid of it.

We're being viewed as angry, entitled, sticking our noses in where we are not wanted, and constantly grumbling about our loss of status and influence. Even our call for religious freedoms is viewed as self-interest. Whose freedoms were we advocating for when we called the shots? Without needing to reach back as far as the Crusades, Christians have been accused of being slow out of the blocks when dealing with systemic racism and all too silent when homosexuals were mistreated and imprisoned. And there's always the spectre of institutional child abuse hanging over the church. So when the cultural, legal and political forces corner and curtail us, they're simply doing their job of protecting everyone else from us, aren't they?

Christians throughout the West are confused and uncertain. Like William Foster standing on Venice Pier, we're astonished that the way we see ourselves is no longer how others see us. And it's all happened in record time.

The Freedom and Joy Program

How did this change happen? How did we get to be the bad guys, and so soon? It would be easy to say that the culture has simply rejected the gospel and is running helter-skelter towards the abyss of a zombie apocalypse of societal collapse, fuelled by sexual orgies and major conflict.

But that does not explain why what is now being offered to us is presented so positively by culture, politics and law. The zombie apocalypse is—stubbornly, maddeningly—not arriving. What is arriving is the hope of a new world that is all glitter and rainbows: a good-news story! Online articles, news stories, movies: these all showcase people who, once lost and confused or struggling with identity because of societally imposed standards, have now been freed by being true to who they feel themselves to be. The former Bruce Jenner, an Olympic champion decathlete and epitome of masculinity, is unveiled to the world as Caitlyn, an example of how we can soar above our pain and hurt and become someone new—and all of our own making. We are being offered a rival gospel: a narrative that seeks first to expose the Christian gospel as bad news, and then to replace it with much-needed good news.

It is this "other" gospel that is driving programs such as the Safe Schools Program in Australia, in which gender fluidity is presented as a solution to bullying problems in state schools. When the program's creator, La Trobe University academic Roz Ward, was challenged about her intent in 2017, she said, "I will never give up fighting for a more free and joyful world".[3]

Freedom and joy in the world. Aren't they our ideas? Is that not our language to describe the future new creation that Christ has won for his people? Melbourne pastor and author Mark Sayers argues in his 2019 book, *Reappearing Church,* that the new reality we are experiencing doesn't create a new set of concepts and ideas to explain itself. It doesn't need to. Christianity in the West, long seen as moribund and empty, has left all of its receptacles and tools behind it as it retreats to the fringes. This new movement has simply picked up and refilled those buckets.

Freedom and human dignity are kingdom concepts. These ideas are grounded in the Bible. They formed the basis of the Christian movement—a movement that swept the world. And they are highly attractive and compelling. Everyone wants the fruit of these ideas.

But the root of these ideas? Not so much. Sayers says that our progressive culture seeks the "kingdom without the King".[4] The ambition is to replicate the kingdom vision of the good life—a future world of human rights, dignity, freedom, love and equality—but all without Jesus at the centre. And, frustratingly for those among us who may wish to see the whole thing come crashing down in order to prove how right we are, this vision appears to be progressing quite well. At least on the surface.

Equality and diversity programs are now par for the course in large corporations. Freedom for sexual minorities is celebrated by secularists everywhere. Emancipation for every marginalised group is showcased across social media. Meanwhile, the church is presented as curmudgeonly, grumpy and downright angry that it is no longer running the freedom and joy program.

Yet while the King has been removed from the kingdom program, the throne has not been vacated. It has been usurped. Who by? Me. You. The individual is now enthroned in this new kingdom.

Politics professor Dale Kuehne has labelled the late modern West the "iWorld". In the traditional world, or "tWorld", our understanding of ourselves and our place in the world was discovered through "relationships of obligation".[5] Society was held together by a recognition that family relationship structures and a commitment to maintaining them—sometimes at personal cost to the individual—was the pathway to flourishing. By contrast, the iWorld locates meaning and purpose within the individual, and relationships of obligation have been replaced by "relationships of choice". Our compass for who we are is not pointed outwards but inwards. We have become the source of meaning—our own meaning—and we only let people into our lives if they affirm and confirm our self-appointed True North.

I cannot emphasise enough how important this shift in how we view relationships is—nor how long it has been in the making. Although it seems just yesterday that we were being told to adopt newly-invented pronouns such as Xi and Xim, the roots of this individual enthronement first grew in the soil of the Enlightenment, several hundred years ago. What we are experiencing today is not the sudden discovery of a new way of looking at the world. Rather, it is the final flowering of a view of humanity that began long before the word "cisgender" ever made it to the humanities departments of our universities.

Canadian philosopher Charles Taylor calls this "the age of authenticity"—an age which traces its roots back through the sexual revolution, past the post-war boom, all the way to the Romantic period that began in the late 18th century.[6] Poets such as William Wordsworth and Lord Byron valued expressive individualism and a deep trust in one's emotional responses. It was untamed nature that they saw as authentic, contrasting it with the soul-destroying strictures of modern life and institutions. In our own age, authenticity is defined by how true you are to yourself; not how true you are to your calling, or your community, or your covenant relationships, but to yourself. This authenticity search has taken on dazzling speed and has, it seems, reached its zenith. The question is, why now?

A Sudden Revolution

The short answer is that massive technological progress is fast-tracking the age of authenticity. While the philosophical shifts have been underway for centuries, we have reached a tipping point today through the incredible transformations that digital technologies have brought to the world and to how we think, live and respond. Lifestyles that were once the domain of the cultural and financial elite are now democratised through the power of the iPhone. Ideas that once took years to filter into the mainstream are conceived, birthed and implemented at breathtaking speed thanks to new forms of instant communication.

Independence and sexual freedom—once only possible for those protected by wealth from their social and relational costs—are now available to everyone. YouTubers and Instagram influencers spread concepts virally, at next to no cost, to teenagers sitting in their bedrooms, racking up huge followings in the process.

One such influencer is Jazz Jennings, who came out as trans while still in single-digit figures age-wise. Jazz's story has been well documented and celebrated by media influencers globally, and Jazz's YouTube channel has millions of views. In 2018, *USA Today* stated, "Jazz Jennings is all smiles after undergoing gender confirmation surgery". That word "confirmation" declares that the contest around identity definitions is over. Yet "complications" following Jazz's surgery remind us that it's not as simple as "becoming who you know you are". Gender-transition surgery is harrowing and mostly irreversible; for many dissatisfied patients, it begins a cycle of repeat surgeries. Years of medical interventions and hormone drugs often follow. Yet rarely are these speed humps on the way to cultural utopia acknowledged.

Jazz's story is an example of how suddenly and comprehensively individualism has been adopted. No sooner is a concept hatched than it is pitched to a world that is always switched on. Guinea pigs are now redundant. Intellectual and moral ideas are now being road-tested by young consumers in real time.

The question for Christians is, how do we meet these challenges? Do we have the tools and the know-how to counter this rival gospel, or will we be swept away with the rest of the cultural foundation stones that once seemed so secure?

Clearly, we have a better gospel—one that does not have to hide behind the euphemism of "complications". It is a gospel which can transform us far more deeply, securely and satisfactorily than any surface work: a gospel of forgiveness and love and acceptance that does not reside in how we feel about our identities.

However, the answer to how we meet these challenges is not settled. As we shall see, an initial strategy that was touted by some Christians as a way to counter this alternative gospel was actually based upon a false reading of where we were headed as a culture. The fact is that our culture is not headed back to an old pre-Christian experience but forward to a new post-Christian one—and one that is hugely hostile to the biblical gospel's vision of humanity. This is a culture and set of beliefs that the church has not encountered before.

Come and Buy

Two decades or so ago, there was excitement among evangelists and those involved in the missional church movement that the world was returning to a pre-Christian period in which the claims of the gospel would be seen afresh—removed from all the traditional cultural associations. I attended meetings in cafés and pubs which discussed the new world we were facing and the opportunities it presented. Our strategy for church planting and evangelism was based on a conviction that postmodernity had levelled the playing field. The Christian faith was now one of many competing spiritual claims in the public square.

Philip Rieff, an American sociologist, has described much of the pre-Christian world as "first culture": a world of many competing gods that were tribal in their allegiances and demands.[7] First culture was not evangelistic. Each god and his or her worshippers kept to their patch.

"Second culture", Rieff argues, changed things. Second culture was monotheistic and evangelistic. Christianity broke down tribal barriers with its commitment to equality across sexes, races and social divisions. It swept the first culture away.

Now, with the eclipse of second-culture values in the

West, we thought we were returning to the first culture—effectively, a pantheon of gods. So the strategy was clear. Christianity would set up a stall alongside everyone else in a free market. And we were confident that, given the chance to offer our wares alongside everyone else's, our products would be more compelling. All we had to do was to strip away the detritus of Christendom that had built up over the centuries—the overt institutionalism, the push for temporal power, the alignment with economic structures that fuelled greed, and the less-than-attractive liturgical forms. The pure and simple claims of Christ could be presented and examined without prejudice by a culture just waiting for some good news. Churches sprang up in households and pubs across the West, ready for an influx of new enquirers.

But that tactic has not worked. Too often, those who began this new movement ended up more like the people in the pub than the people in the pub ended up like Jesus. Often this was led from the top, as early missional leaders such as Rob Bell moved from a stated theological humility to what can only be classed as heretical viewpoints.

Many others were left feeling burnt out, seeing little fruit for all of their endeavours and shattered by the suburban grind of mortgages, small children, jobs in the city and disconnected weekday lives. Some returned, chastened but relieved, to traditional churches, where they enacted some of the things they'd learned. Some left church for good. Others left Jesus for good—not all, but far too many.

The reason this happened is becoming clearer. What we are experiencing now is not a return to pre-Christianity but a move forward to something new: a post-Christian reality. It is what Philip Rieff labelled "third culture". First and second cultures had something that third culture does not possess: a spiritual or transcendent order that gave shape to the social order. People related to God or the gods through social and cultural structures, in which temples and other holy locations, families and households, liturgical calendars and seasons all pointed to realities beyond themselves. The patterns established on earth were exactly that: patterns of something transcendent.

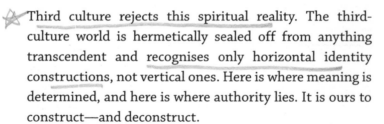

Third culture rejects this spiritual reality. The third-culture world is hermetically sealed off from anything transcendent and recognises only horizontal identity constructions, not vertical ones. Here is where meaning is determined, and here is where authority lies. It is ours to construct—and deconstruct.

Simply put, when we decided we were headed back to a pre-Christian pagan view of the world, which would give us the kind of hearing we had back in the early centuries, we misread the data. Unlike the first culture, this third culture is highly evangelistic and actively hostile to second-culture values. It has features and inbuilt bugs that render it resistant to many of the tactics employed in pre-Christian days that we were confident would work again.

We'll Take It From Here

Secular cultural commentators have read the data better than Christians have. In his book *The Madness of Crowds,* British author and commentator Douglas Murray, who is gay and an atheist, says that we have been living through "a period of more than a quarter of a century in which all of our grand narratives have collapsed".[8] But, of course, nature abhors a vacuum. Murray goes on to say this: "Western democracies today could not simply remain the first people in recorded history to have absolutely no explanation for what we are doing here, and no story to give life purpose".[9]

At exactly the same period in history that the traditional Western narrative, steeped as it was in the Christian framework, fell from influence, the rise of digital technologies and social media provided a platform for other, nimbler and more compelling narrators to fill the void, and to do so quickly. Hello Silicon Valley. Murray points out the speed at which a handful of businesses in Southern California have not only gained "the power … to direct what most people in the world know, think and say, but [also] a business model which has accurately been described as relying on 'finding customers ready to pay to modify someone else's behaviour'".[10] The primary behaviour modification that these platforms are committed to is the embedding of a "new metaphysics in our societies; a new religion, if you will".

Even an atheist such as Murray recognises that what we are facing is a new religion—one built on commitment to individual autonomy and celebration of personal authenticity at any cost. It is a religion that finds ultimate meaning in the self, to counter the gospel that finds ultimate meaning in God and his King, Jesus Christ.

This post-Christian culture has at its disposal the tools, terminologies and categories of the Christian world, but utilises them in ways that are hostile to the Christian faith. Minority groups within the West appear to do community just as tightly, if not more so, than many Christian communities. Social-justice campaigns which serve the poor the way that Christians do, can at the same time be extremely hostile to the claims of the Christian faith.

Academic and writer Rosaria Champagne Butterfield observes that when she became a Christian, she found to her initial dismay that the lesbian community she moved *from* was tighter in many ways than the community she moved *to*.[11] That is not the sum total of her experience, and Butterfield grew to realise that community and hospitality, *in and of themselves,* were not enough. But we cannot dismiss the iWorld by saying that we do what they do, only better—as we could in Roman times. We've done such a good job at "christianising" our culture, giving it rich and fulfilling categories, that the new religion can say, "Thanks very much, we'll take it from here".

And that is what it is doing. This new religious reality is even now offering a kind of post-Christian discipleship program that directly challenges the authoritative claims of the gospel. It does so with such an alluring aesthetic that it will even draw away some from within the church—anyone not grounded in the cross-shaped gospel of Jesus.

My church network has traditionally only held evening services. That's popular for many people in our setting. But it's also resulted in what we call "second-service Christians": those who attend a morning service elsewhere as their primary church and then come to us in the evening. It's hard to get someone to serve and give and be discipled to be more like Christ when they are a second-service Christian.

But the reality today is that all Christians are second-service Christians. All of us are immersed in a highly effective discipleship program offered by our culture Monday through Saturday. In everything, from our phones to Netflix to advertising and news items, we are being offered a discipleship program that invites us to a completely different way of life, mediated to us through a dazzling array of images, sounds, stories and suggestions. In response, our church gatherings on Sundays must offer discipleship programs that are deeper, richer and more compelling than those offered by the culture. As God's people we are tasked with laundering one discipleship program *out* of ourselves first, before we can even begin to launder the gospel discipleship program *in*.

So, the post-Christian culture puts twin pressures on us. How do we offer the true and better gospel to those outside the church who view it as not only wrong but possibly dangerous? And how do we ensure that the alternative

29

gospel does not entice and draw away those among us who are being charmed by its online claims 24/7?

I do believe that what we have in the gospel is the most liberating, hope-filled news that the world has ever seen. Nothing has changed that conviction in me. So how do we recognise and challenge the counterfeit gospel? The same way that law-enforcement agencies train their staff to recognise counterfeit banknotes: not by examining every detail of a fake ten-dollar bill but by becoming completely familiar with legitimate currency. We must turn to the truth of the Bible to get our direction.

Endnotes

[1] "David Mackereth: Christian doctor loses trans beliefs case", *BBC News* 2 Oct. 2019 (https://www.bbc.co.uk/news/uk-england-birmingham-49904997) (accessed 18 Aug. 2020).

[2] Tom Holland, *Dominion* (Little, Brown, 2019), p 524.

[3] Roz Ward, "I will never give up fighting for a more free and joyful world", *The Guardian* 1 Sep. 2017 (www.theguardian.com/commentisfree/2017/sep/01/roz-ward-i-will-never-give-up-fighting-for-a-more-free-and-joyful-world) (accessed 30 Jan. 2020).

[4] Mark Sayers, *Reappearing Church* (Moody, 2019), p 24.

[5] Dale Kuehne, *Sex and the iWorld* (Baker Academic, 2009), p 35.

[6] Charles Taylor, *A Secular Age* (Belknap Press, 2007), p 473-504.

[7] Philip Rieff, *My Life Among the Deathworks* (University of Virginia Press, 2006).

[8] Douglas Murray, *The Madness of Crowds* (Bloomsbury, 2019), p 1.

[9] *The Madness of Crowds*, p 2.

[10] *The Madness of Crowds*, p 2, referencing Jason Lanier, *Ten Arguments for Deleting Your Social Media Accounts Right Now* (Bodley Head, 2018).

[11] Rosaria Butterfield, *Openness Unhindered* (Crown and Covenant, 2015), 71% on Kindle.

2. Why the Surprise?

The Bible tells us to expect hostility as Christians. I say this now—before we get to the specific narratives of the rival gospel we are facing—because the cultural shifts and challenging responses that many in the Western church face today can be discombobulating if we do not have this reality locked away. If the church is bred on a diet of self-help books that try to convince us that God's intention is to make our lives as smooth as possible, we will be suckers in a hostile world. No wonder we become confused, angry or despairing when the culture is throwing rotten tomatoes, not rose petals, at us.

Instead we need to take a serious look at what the Bible tells us to expect.

When famed Antarctic explorer Ernest Shackleton was looking to build a team for his dangerous and daring polar expedition at the start of the 20th century, it's said that he placed an advertisement in a newspaper with the following words:

"Men wanted for hazardous journey. Low wages, bitter cold, long hours of complete darkness. Safe return doubtful. Honour and recognition in event of success."

Apparently some 5,000 men replied. I doubt if any of these 5,000 asked about the fringe benefit arrangements, or whether there would be good coffee. None was left in any doubt by Shackleton that this was going to be arduous, lonely and perhaps fatal. All the hardships were in plain sight in the advertisement. Shackleton was not interested in signing up men through a bait-and-switch method. He established early on what type of person would be required for the journey and made sure that no one would be able to complain later when it got tough—as it inevitably would.

Everything that is hazardous *about* the gospel is in plain sight *in* the gospel. Everything that we should be aware of—the pitfalls, the dangers, the opposition, the pushback, the persecution—is right there not only in Scripture's words about the gospel, but in the gospel action itself. The cross of the Lord Jesus is proof that anyone who wants to be a disciple of Jesus must face the possibility of deep hostility from the powers of this age. If we are going to sit in the cultural stocks, facing the jeering crowds with any sense of joy or confidence, then we need instead to take on the same resilient attitude as Shackleton's men. Except, of course, for this one proviso, and it's one that makes all the difference: unlike for those men, a safe return is guaranteed for the people of God. That is God's constant promise to his people in the Scriptures.

The story of God's people throughout the Bible is always one of "suffer now, glory later". Always. Of course, Jesus himself is the template—announcing in Luke 24 v 26 that the path of suffering is a prerequisite for God's anointed one prior to glory. There is no "glory now, never suffer" option for those who would remain faithful to God.

Significantly, Jesus' explanation of his suffering in Luke 24 made use of "all the Scriptures" (v 27). Perhaps he referred to the suffering of King David, the proto-Messiah, who was cast out into the desert with his men in fear of his own life, and who only returned much later to Jerusalem to be crowned in glory. Or the most famous sufferer of all, Job, who even in his darkest moments asserted that even if his flesh was destroyed, he would see God (Job 19 v 26). Perhaps Jesus spoke of the poignant story of Hannah, Samuel's mother, who suffered barrenness and mockery before she gave birth to the man who would be Israel's great prophet. Hannah's song in 1 Samuel 2 explores that very theme of reversal, where the rich become poor and the poor rich, the mother of many is reduced to none and the barren woman rejoices with a son. The story of the Bible shows that "suffer now, glory later" is the norm for God's people.

Knowing this to be the case should enable us to cope with whatever is being thrown at us in the secular culture—and not only to cope but to do so with joy. That lesson is often learned through pain. But be comforted: the apostle Peter learned the same lesson through even more pain. He expected "glory now" when the disciples arrived in Jerusalem, despite Jesus' insistence that suffering was coming (Mark 8 v 27-33). Those hopes were painfully dashed when Jesus was arrested—leading Peter to deny even knowing the Lord who had chosen him. Peter's shameful part in the story of the cross proves that at the time, unlike Shackleton's men, he was neither resilient enough nor ready for a hazardous journey. He could not see the necessity of "suffer now, glory later".

Taking the Shackleton Option

But how things changed! Jesus was raised from the dead, to the astonishment of the disciples; Peter was graciously and powerfully restored in his relationship to the One he had denied; Jesus taught his disciples about his kingdom for 40 days prior to his ascension; the Holy Spirit was poured out on the disciples at Pentecost. These events emboldened the disciples to face any hazards that would come their way for the sake of the gospel. Right at the outset of the church's story, the same disciples who ran from any hint of danger on the night of Jesus' betrayal were ecstatic as they walked away from a beating. Not because they had suffered but because of why they had suffered:

*[They] left ... rejoicing because they had been counted worthy
of suffering disgrace for the Name. (Acts 5 v 41)*

The "Name"—the name of Jesus Christ—shaped
everything the disciples did for the rest of their lives. Every
sorrow, every joy, every trouble, every persecution, every
believer was transformed by the resurrected Jesus. And
everywhere they went, whoever they shared the message
with, they shared the reality of suffering as well. It's no
surprise that years later, when writing to churches around
the Roman Empire who were facing scorn and rejection by
their culture for following a king other than Caesar, Peter
took the "Shackleton option". He wrote these words:

*Dear friends, do not be surprised at the fiery ordeal that has
come on you to test you, as though something strange were
happening to you. But rejoice inasmuch as you participate in
the sufferings of Christ, so that you may be overjoyed when
his glory is revealed. If you are insulted because of the name of
Christ, you are blessed, for the Spirit of glory and of God rests
on you. If you suffer, it should not be as a murderer or thief or
any other kind of criminal, or even as a meddler. However, if
you suffer as a Christian, do not be ashamed, but praise God
that you bear that name. For it is time for judgment to begin
with God's household; and if it begins with us, what will the
outcome be for those who do not obey the gospel of God? And,
"If it is hard for the righteous to be saved, what will become
of the ungodly and the sinner?" So then, those who suffer
according to God's will should commit themselves to their
faithful Creator and continue to do good. (1 Peter 4 v 12-19)*

Peter's words highlight three aspects of this hostility: the reality of it, our reaction to it, and the reason behind it.

Don't Be Surprised

The hostile culture in the West is our Shackleton moment. Peter tells his readers not to be surprised at the fiery ordeal because it's actually not strange. In fact, it is to be expected. As we read 1 Peter, it's clear that what the Christians were experiencing back then was not the full-scale persecution and being fed to the lions that we commonly think of when we think of the persecution of the early church. That came later. Rather, they were maligned for not joining the wild partying (4 v 4), and "insulted because of the name of Christ" (4 v 14). 2 v 12 tells us that they were "accuse[d] ... of doing wrong" and 3 v 16 that people spoke "maliciously" about them. This was good old garden-variety abuse and scorn for being followers of Jesus.

In those days they didn't have Twitter, Facebook, Instagram and a host of websites through which to deliver the abuse and scorn, but there is little difference in content between what they were experiencing and what we are experiencing in the West today. Signing up to Team Jesus in AD 50 resulted in the same cultural rejection as it does now.

Jesus said the same thing. He told his disciples, "If the world hates you, keep in mind that it hated me first" (John 15 v 18). Nothing in the Gospels gives any indication that there will be a blanket acceptance of Jesus and his message—it's just the opposite. Jesus' most important parable, the one that he said unpacks all of the parables (Mark 4 v 11-12), proves it. The parable of the sower—or, more pointedly, the parable of the soils—in Mark 4 is Jesus' explanation of his own ministry. First, there will be those who reject the message out of hand, like when birds eat the seed. Second, there will be those who, because of trouble or persecution, fall away—that's the rocky ground. Third, there will be those who are swept away by what this world offers—the thorns. Finally, there will be those who accept the message and bear fruit—the good soil.

Jesus nailed humanity's reactions to his ministry right there. All four categories have remained throughout church history. In some locations and times, one or more of the soils will come to the fore, such as when there is a revival and many people believe and bear fruit; or when wealth in a nation draws people away from humility and dependence on God. In our time it is that second soil, the rocky ground of persecution and trouble, which confronts us through a hostile social media, Twitter pile-ons and online trolling. If we are not prepared for this, then standing up for Jesus and his truth will seem too difficult, and we, like that second soil, will reject the word.

This is especially true when others are giving in, falling away from Jesus' teachings and being openly embraced by the culture that was once hostile to them. It's one thing to stand united and put up with rejection by the world; it's another thing altogether when someone breaks ranks.

One painful recent example is megachurch pastor Joshua

Harris, author of the bestselling book *I Kissed Dating Goodbye,* which ushered in the purity movement of the 2000s. Harris was famous by the age of 21 and a senior pastor of a major church by his early thirties. Yet in a carefully crafted series of Instagram statements in 2019, he first announced the end of his own marriage, then the end of his own faith, and then an open apology and celebration of the LGBTQI lifestyle.

There was the whiff of a conversion experience in Harris's media feeds, and a warm embrace by the liberal media upon his announcements. Harris would say his eyes were opened and many would call his journey progress. We would say, with tears in our eyes, that this is a tragedy; and, with the humility that comes from knowing that only God's grace keeps us from walking the same way, we would add that his heart was rocky soil—though there's always hope he'll turn again to Christ. One thing is certain, though: right now, he no longer has to put up with the maligning and reviling of the world. He is liberated from the fiery ordeal that Peter speaks about. For many others, as the cultural temperature goes through the roof, that liberation is an increasingly attractive option. But 1 Peter 4 calls us to face the reality of persecution and not blink.

Do Be Overjoyed

If our reaction shouldn't be surprise, then what should it be? Rejoicing! It's astonishing how often in the Scriptures the command to rejoice amid suffering pops up. It's not just in 1 Peter 4. Jesus calls his disciples to rejoice when they are spoken badly of (Luke 6 v 22-23); Paul's letter to the Philippians is laced with calls to rejoice; the writer to the Hebrews reminds his readers how they joyfully endured "the confiscation of [their] property" (Hebrews 10 v 34); and James begins his letter with a call for joy in the midst of suffering for Jesus (James 1 v 2). Whatever else may be said to be common to the Christian community throughout history, joy is certainly front and centre.

Where does this joy spring from? Not circumstances. Never circumstances. Peter links the rejoicing he calls for with the reality that persecution is actually a sharing in the sufferings of Jesus (1 Peter 4 v 13). Just as Jesus was vindicated by the resurrection, those who suffer for him will be vindicated by his return. So it's "when his glory is revealed" that they'll be overjoyed—and this certain hope leads them to rejoice even now, in anticipation. For the Christian, joy in the present is always future-focused.

This is worth bearing in mind in a world which lives in a perpetual state of "now", especially the online world that feeds on and then regurgitates anger towards injustices, actual or otherwise. It is easy for Christians to be swept up into this anger. It isn't hard to think of examples of injustices experienced by Christians in workplaces or universities, just for holding to beliefs that were considered perfectly normal a mere five minutes ago. And there is nothing wrong with defending the long-held freedoms that Christianity helped to give to our culture—the very culture that is now jettisoning the Christian framework. There are insightful and gifted individuals and organisations working to ensure that these freedoms are not lost. But too often there is also a sense of rage among Christians, giving the impression that what is going on is a zero-sum game—that if we don't win this culture war, everything is over. That is

how earthly politics works, not God's kingdom.

The New Testament documents were written in a context where Roman imperial power held sway. But Paul could call on Christians in Rome to be subject to those governing authorities (Romans 13 v 1) because God is the ultimate authority. The Scriptures clearly hold out our ultimate hope—and the joy that accompanies it—in the return of the resurrected Jesus. His suffering is presented as the template for us to follow, knowing that suffering now will lead to glory later. This world is *not* all there is.

Peter is so sure of this future inevitability that he speaks of it in the present tense: "If you are insulted because of the name of Christ, you are blessed" (1 Peter 4 v 14). The present presence of God's Spirit guarantees the glory to

come, whatever the current experience. Anger or outrage are sure signs that the future joy guaranteed to us has fallen off our radars as we are insulted or sidelined or scorned. Reacting with joy is a better reflection of reality.

A Good Reason to Suffer

It would be easy to stick to the surface and say that the reason we are experiencing this hostile cultural pushback is because the Christian framework is being rejected and the ethical bedrock upon which our Western civilisation was built is being undermined. To some extent, that is true.

But Peter highlights a deeper, underlying truth. What we are experiencing is God's work of purifying his church. Peter puts it in stark terms when he says, "For it is time for judgment to begin with God's household" (1 Peter 4 v 17). What does Peter mean by that? It may sound to us as if he is saying that God is specifically angry at his people for some serious sin, and that the pushback from our culture is therefore his way of punishing us. But that cannot be right, because it does not align with what the Bible teaches about God's judgment. Jesus took the punishment of sin upon himself on the cross. When he cried out, "It is finished!" he meant that he had done the work required of him: the sin that requires judgment had been dealt with once and for all.

Besides, understanding "judgment" here as punishment is clearly at odds with how Peter speaks about the churches he is writing to. The language of blessing, inheritance, salvation and royal priesthood peppers this letter, jarring with any reading that has the church sitting under judgment for sin. Peter contrasts the household of God with "those who do not obey the gospel of God" (v 17), killing off any charge that the cultural hostility his readers—and, by inference, we—experience is primarily because of disobedience.

What is more likely is that "judgment" is being used here in the sense of refining and proving. Peter, chastened as he was by his own failure to accept suffering on the way to Calvary, states elsewhere, "You may have had to suffer grief in all kinds of trials. These have come so that the proven genuineness of your faith ... may result in praise, glory and honour when Jesus Christ is revealed" (1 Peter 1 v 6-7). The suffering that his readers are experiencing is not punishment for sin but rather the purifying process that all of God's people undergo. The struggles we are experiencing as the culture turns against us are an opportunity for God to refine us—both individually and as a church—in order to bring glory to God through our joyful obedience in the midst of suffering.

The Wrong Reason to Suffer

The primary reason we know that the suffering Peter is talking about is not a punishment for disobedience is because the text clearly differentiates between two types of suffering. 1 Peter 4 v 15 bears repeating:

> *If you suffer, it should not be as a murderer or thief or any other kind of criminal, or even as a meddler.*

There is a right way to suffer, and it is infused with joy. There is a wrong way to suffer, and it is infused with shame. From murderer to meddler, Peter works his way down through a list of sins that bring shame from the culture. This time, the shame is thoroughly deserved. And he holds out the possibility that Christians could suffer for these sins if they are not careful to avoid them.

In later chapters we will explore some areas of public life in which the Christian church, although far from guilty of murder, may have been complicit in sins that have brought rightful shame upon us. Certainly, some of the anger that Christians have faced in recent years is a result of actions that could fit the description "meddling". If we are chippy or rude or deliberately go out of our way to provoke those with whom we disagree, we can hardly turn around and claim that we are suffering for the sake of the gospel.

 Jesus is the One who did not threaten when he suffered (1 Peter 2 v 23); Peter cannot point to himself as an example. In Gethsemane, Peter picked up a sword and swung it, cutting off a man's ear (Luke 22 v 47-51)—if his aim had been straighter, he might have been guilty of murder. Jesus restored the man's ear, then later restored Peter. If we confess our own ungodly reactions to the hostility we often face from the culture, we too can be restored. In fact, we can be assured of it.

Peter learned his lesson the hard way and wants others to avoid the same shame and sorrow that he experienced. This is something I have struggled with myself, especially in my public ministry of theological and cultural blogging and interacting on social media with those who are hostile towards the Christian faith. On more than one occasion I have been convicted by God's Spirit to apologise publicly to people towards whom I have been less than charitable. The sin of meddling is easy as we cruise our way through Facebook, putting in a snipe here and a less-than-godly putdown there, and generally looking to "one-up" those with whom we disagree. It's also easy in offline conversations: how many of us have used what knowledge we have to win arguments at dinner gatherings and family-gathering occasions like Christmas or Thanksgiving?

The temptation to meddle and argue for the sake of it is only going to increase as hostility ramps up and the Christian faith finds itself under more scrutiny culturally, legally and politically. Although it can be hard to do, and although we live in a reactionary time, our first instinct should be to expect hostility rather than be surprised at it, and to rejoice even when all "tweeters" speak evil of us on account of our faith.

The apostle Peter had been a fear-driven and angry man who lashed out at those who came to arrest Jesus. He became a pastor who advised those living in hostile conditions not to return evil for evil, not to revile when reviled, and instead to be like Jesus and entrust themselves to the One who judges justly. If that change was possible in someone like Peter, then it is completely possible for us. God is speaking to us today through what he said to Peter's first audience then.

With that in mind, let's move from "then" to today and examine exactly what this hostility looks like in our own situation.

---

3. Binary Beige Versus Diverse Rainbows

When the BBC produced a series of videos for primary schools that announced that there were at least 100 genders, the UK's national broadcaster found itself making the news, not merely reporting it.

The nine videos created by BBC Teach include a mock-up Q and A session in which a young boy asks his teacher how many genders there are, before being congratulated on asking "a really, really exciting question". The scene cuts to another teacher explaining to other children that "We know that we have got male and female, but there are over 100, if not more, gender identities now".[1]

For some, this is yet one more sign that the culture has gone crazy. The number of genders is climbing at a dizzying rate, with university humanities departments leading the way in discovering them, and biology departments affirming them. For some, this is proof that we're committing intellectual suicide. And it has pastoral implications: the BBC's videos were accused of creating further confusion for vulnerable pre-pubescent young people.

But for others, this acknowledgement by a respected broadcaster shows that we are heading towards a wonderful, liberated future—one that we have been denied so far by a beige, repressive view about sex and gender. The BBC is laying the groundwork for a better world: a rainbow world, in which each person can truly be themselves and in which harmful social constrictions, formerly used to stifle true difference and creativity, will be abolished.

For too long, so this story goes, diversity has been repressed by a suffocating conformity that we are now discovering bears less relationship to science than it had claimed. The binary world of male and female, in which sex and gender matched, is being exposed as culturally harmful. Now, anyone who argues for the existence of only two genders, or that sex is inherent, will discover they are on the wrong side of history. And not only the wrong side, the *harmful* side.

This "liberation" of sex and gender promises to end the abuse of power that the church and other institutions inflicted on those who did not conform. The world of binary beige is behind us. The joyful rainbow hues of true diversity lie ahead.

The speed of change has caught many people, especially Christians, by surprise. Yet it is not the pace of change that is most confronting. The true challenge for Christians, and indeed for many secular people, is the level of hostility around this topic.

This is no longer a discussion. Ideas which were confined to academics and activists a decade ago are now declared to be not simply mainstream, but the *only permitted* ideas from this point on. Challenging these new convictions is not merely considered misguided but bad; to do so is thought to risk causing suicides and mental-health issues. Corporations now punish individuals and organisations who refuse to recognise the growing list of genders.

Two Mistakes Christians Made

How did this happen? And how did Christians find themselves so distanced from cultural, legal, political and even scientific sentiment?

The first mistake was the one I outlined in chapter 1: assuming that the post-Christian secular public square would be a neutral venue, a space for everyone, where all sorts of ideas would be discussed freely. We prepared our strategies for an open market, never realising that huge tariffs would be imposed on anyone selling their wares in the public space.

The public space is not neutral. Why not? Because secularism is not neutral. What has been pitched as a bedrock "values-free" framework actually operates under huge assumptions.

Secularism pitches itself, as the philosopher Charles Taylor argues, as a "subtraction story": what's left over after dogma has been removed.[2] A secular age, we were assured, would be detached from old myths and ideologies. But everyone needs a framework to live by. The old ideologies were replaced by the assertion that we determine our own identities. This is itself a dogma, an ideology, yet one that is oblivious to itself.

Here's how this works for sex and gender. Sex is what we are "assigned" at birth, generally a binary: male or female. But note, it is "assigned". It is given to you at birth when you are powerless to say otherwise. (Even this is changing. Legal jurisdictions throughout the West are permitting birth certificates with "unassigned" next to the question of sex.)

If the bad news is that sex is assigned, then the good news—the "gospel" if you wish—is that you are now free to determine your gender. Your gender is the real you and cannot be imposed externally by hostile and controlling narratives, especially not religious ones.

This leads to the final piece of the gender jigsaw: gender identity trumps assigned sex. Indeed, gender redefines sex—hence the rise of transgenderism.

The speed of this change has blindsided Christians. But not just the speed: also the almost religious intensity with which this view is held. It is a deeply cherished, quasi-spiritual belief, and too many of us have realised this belatedly.

We assumed that sex and gender was a sidebar discussion, unimportant to questions of deep identity. These minor topics could be set aside while the deeper matters of religion and spirituality were discussed. Category error right there! This was our second mistake. It turns out that these matters are deeply spiritual and central to the quest for meaning. Gender identity is now the deepest, most important reality about the self—central to the new secular religion.

This new truth is reinforced by changing usage of terms, as observed by transgender person Debbie Hayton in an article in February 2020 in the conservative journal *Quillette*. Hayton has gender dysphoria and lives as a woman, yet rejects the view that gender identity trumps biological sex: "I may have transitioned socially, medically and surgically, but I am as male now as I was the day I was born".[3]

But this is a minority viewpoint, Hayton points out, for in our culture words such as "man" and "woman" do not mean what they used to, and are being changed even in legal codes across a wide range of jurisdictions. The basis for this is the following idea:

"We all have an innate gender identity—analogous to the divine spark that religious adherents claim is lodged within us—which determines whether we are a man, a woman or non-binary."

Note the use of the phrase "divine spark". Hayton's point is that this is a religious clash. That is why it is so heated. That is why, in the context of a materialist world in which humans are just meat, synapses and hormones, the idea of being "born in the wrong body" has traction. The language of the soul has returned.

Such language would have been scorned by psychiatrists and other mental-health professionals just two decades ago, as it would have opened the door to the non-materialist worldview their professions had spent decades shutting out. Now? Those who publicly reject it do so at risk of being struck off the register. To challenge this new religion's terminology and assumptions is to be accused of hate speech, or refused a work contract or entry into a professional association. Many professions may soon be closed to those who will not sign off on the increasingly philosophy-driven statements of employers. The temptation, of course, will be to sign off just to get the job.

Yet even this is being touted as good news. The mental health of those challenging the traditional views on sex and gender is more important than whether a Christian psychiatrist keeps their job. Every revolutionary omelette requires a few cracked eggs.

It is not just Christians experiencing the hostility. Harry Potter author, JK Rowling, in coming to the defence of Maya Forstater, a woman who had lost her job over a public statement that biological sex was fixed, tweeted the following:

"Dress however you please
Call yourself whatever you like
Sleep with any consenting adult who'll have you
Live your best life in peace and security
But force women out of their jobs for stating that sex is real?"

She finished with two hashtags: #IStandWithMaya and #ThisIsNotADrill.

Immediately, the twitterati demanded that Rowling's books be removed from schools and libraries. Some activists bemoaned the loss of Hogwarts as a "safe place" where, as children, they could truly be themselves.

In response, British journalist Brendan O'Neill made this call:

"The only way this woke censorship and persecution of disobedient women will be countered is if more individuals and institutions stand up to it. Everyone must now say what has, surreally, become unsayable: that sex is real, that sex is immutable, and that if you are born male, you will die male, regardless of what you do to yourself."[4]

Yet O'Neill's call to arms will generally be ignored, even if people share his convictions. The emotional cost of standing up—not to say the financial, relational and professional costs—seems too high. Rowling has doubled down on the matter, even in light of this public scorching, scoffing at a global health campaign for using the term "people who menstruate" in place of the word "women". The actors she made stars, including Daniel Radcliffe, were united in both condemning her and insisting that any person who claims to be a woman is a woman. If those with money and cultural traction such as Rowling can be cancelled, what chance is there for those of us who are always two lost wage packets from financial ruin?

The cost will be higher again for Christians. As those who know that counting the cost of following Jesus is part of the package, we're not simply standing up for biological truth but for theological truth. In that sense we would not line up with Rowling, who is not arguing for anything beyond a different view of how to live out individualised and autonomous lives. Unlike her, our concerns centre around something bigger than us and beyond us.

We need to go back to the beginning to see why.

Creation: A Binary Account

Past conflicts about the opening of Genesis focused on the literal understanding of creation. Were there six actual days or is that a literary device? Recently, the argument has shifted from science to philosophy and from solar settings to sexual ones. As a result, the first chapters of Genesis are in the firing line once again, this time because of their binary understanding of God's created order.

It is not merely humans who are created binary; the *whole* of creation in Genesis 1 and 2 is binary. We see equal opposites everywhere: light and dark; day and night; land and sea; earth and heavens; animal and human; male and female; and—most significantly—Creator and creature. The binary nature of male and female is embedded within a binary system culminating in the most binary relationship of all: the one between the God who created all things and the humans he created.

Land is not sea, day is not night, and creatures are not Creator. That's how these binary distinctions work. God calls this ordered pattern "very good".

But God says it is "not good" that Adam be alone, demonstrating the fact that one puzzle piece is missing: a creature who will fulfil God's design for creation and Adam's desire for companionship. Another human is introduced: a human, but *not* a man. Eve is Adam's equal and his opposite. The creation is announced as complete when this binary "other" is brought to the man and he praises her.

Critically, "good" or "very good" is not simply pointing to the moral nature of the creation. It is a declaration that the creation is operating according to the manner in which God intended it to. This should, as a result, lead to *human and creational flourishing.*

A Tale of Two Views

This is the dilemma we face today. Which view of the world, which practices of humanity, will lead to human and creational flourishing? Will it be the binary pattern of Genesis 1 – 2? Or are these chapters a hindrance and threat to the joyous new world being promised to us: one in which the toxic restrictions of assigned sex and binary gender are cast off? It's a deeply religious battle, because it is not just personal choices that are at stake. This is about the purpose of humanity and the identity of the created order.

The gender binary fits into God's wider pattern of equal opposites. It is the Christian conviction that to move away from these binary relationships will not only risk human flourishing but lead to human destruction. That is why this is a step up from the concerns of the secular Rowlings and O'Neills.

Our primary concern is—or ought to be—not that our personal lives will become harder, nor that our children will have to grow up in a hostile sexual setting, nor even that we might lose our jobs because of our faith. Rather, it is that the rapid rejection of this binary understanding of the world will both destroy and be used to destroy those who have been made in the image of God. It is a rejection of God himself.

Human flourishing is at risk because of this rejection. More than that: as we read in Romans 1, God's wrath is kindled against those who reject his good creation plan. The breaking of the binary "code" in Genesis is presented by Paul as a double whammy. He sees evidence of humanity's rejection of God's good order both in the worshipping and serving of "created things rather than the Creator" (v 25) and in the sexual boundary between male and female being crossed (v 26-27). He also sees these things as evidence of God's wrath itself. God hands people over to what will prevent them from flourishing, as a portent of future and final judgment. Anyone want to sign up for sharing those twin truths with their friends?

This is confronting. It is confronting to us whose friends and family reject this truth in thought and practice. And it is confronting to our faith because it is a basic building block of what we say is a better story. The story of God's design and humanity's rejection of that design is a critical part of our gospel pronouncement—at a time when such pronouncements are viewed as toxic and as hate speech.

Yet it is also confronting because the "zombie apocalypse" of post-Christian societal breakdown is not yet evident. Our story appears to lack plausibility. The diversity rainbow is presented as the right story instead: the one which the West must adopt in order to press on towards a brighter future.

The success of this story in our culture is partly due to the active suppression of dissent. The voices of those who have left that rainbow narrative behind, or who have been bruised and hurt by it, are not welcome in the conversation. Those who do leave find themselves ostracised and scorned on social media as traitors. Meanwhile, health practitioners who see the less-than-happy results of this social movement are nervous to speak out in case they are labelled as unworthy of their profession.

In the midst of all this, Christian psychiatrist Glynn Harrison makes this call on the church:

"It is time to recover our confidence that the Christian vision for sex, marriage and family also conveys social and relational goods that can bring blessing and flourishing to all ... we need to share what we have found, for the sake of all those whose lives have been hollowed out by pornography, promiscuity, trafficking and by the fruitless pursuit of self-fulfilment. We have been given life for the world and we cannot keep it to ourselves."[5]

Yet many of us *have* lost our confidence. Many of us *do* want to keep this vision to ourselves. The cost of sharing the Christian vision seems too high, the risk of sharing it too bracing. We have lost confidence as we watch church sexual scandals and abuse make headlines; as we struggle with our own sexual sin and temptations; and as we see the anguish of those who have left the faith because of this issue.

And to top it off, some churches and denominations are opting out of the Christian vision and joining the rainbow one. When they do, they are welcomed into the public square with open arms. It is beginning to feel lonely. When will this thing bottom out?

What Can We Do?

It is tempting to think that the best solution is to push hard to repeal laws that are foisting these things upon us. Or to create enclaves where we can practise our faith in gated compounds with limited cultural interaction. Such strategies are either naïve about the culture or naïve about the church. The cultural changes are not yet for turning, and they are increasingly intrusive. Besides, historically the church has never flourished when it retreats to disengagement and quietism. Sin finds a way into our self-made Gardens of Eden.

That last point is a reminder that while there is no way back to Eden, we should not have been looking for one in the first place. Eden was never God's final intention for human flourishing. Our hope is not in reconstruction but in re-creation. Central to the confidence that Harrison calls us to is the conviction that our *primary* identity is no more grounded in heterosexual binary relationships than it is in the 100 genders or more of the BBC.

In the same way that Genesis tells us that humans were made in the image of God during creation, the gospel also tells us that believers have been remade in the image of Christ. We draw our identity from Christ. The core of our identity—the place where our meaning lies—does not come from sex or gender but from who we have been declared and recreated to be in Jesus.

Christ alone, as the Creator and Sustainer of the church, is central to our ability to model a counter culture that is neither reactionary and angry in the face of rapidly disappearing notions of sex and gender nor simply apes the culture's championing of the individual and his or her desires.

We need to ask how we may have unwittingly bought into the framework that self-fulfilment leads to flourishing, even while we reject its more startling conclusions. Our response ought to be as shocking to JK Rowling and to Brendan O'Neill as it is to the schools programmes department of the BBC.

And the way we live must be shocking in a way that is also compelling. It must raise questions for those looking on— questions such as, *If their way of thinking about sexuality and individual expression is so wrong, how come their lives look so good?* Or, *If they're supposedly given over to hate speech, how come they serve and love their enemies?* Or, *Why is their speech so measured when they are scorned on social media?* Or (most perturbingly to a culture that views personal sexual freedom as our primary identity marker), *Why are their marriages strong, their single people chaste, and their same-sex-attracted people so fulfilled by non-sexual relationships?*

We have some way to go, but if we ground our identity together in Christ, at least we're headed in the right direction.

None of this is to say that there is no place for pushing back against the sexual mores of the culture. But the more we understand that our flourishing lies in the future fulfilment of the Genesis creation story, the more confident we will be now. The old creation was never our goal; the new creation is. God is fulfilling his purposes for the new creation just as surely as he fulfilled his purposes for the first creation.

So what is my advice when the work fundraiser is in aid of an LGBTQI cause, you're invited to a gay wedding, or your kids come home from school telling you there are 100 genders or more? In the first place, it's simply to take a step back and remind yourself of what your identity is. That is the starting point for any godly response to these conundrums.

There is much to say about these matters and there are no easy solutions. But we can be confident that there is a far richer, more colourful vision of flourishing available to us than what any gender identity program offers. The final chapters of this book will explore this in greater detail, with three practical strategies that will both strengthen us as God's people and be attractive to outsiders. For now, let's remember that when someone reaches the end of the promised sexual and gender rainbow, they are sure to discover that fool's gold can glitter as brightly as the real thing.

Endnotes

[1] www.bbc.co.uk/teach/class-clips-video/rse-ks2-identity-understanding-sexual-and-gender-identities/zfqrhbk (accessed 30 Dec. 2019).

[2] *A Secular Age*, p 22.

[3] Debbie Hayton, "I may have gender dysphoria. But I still prefer to base my life on biology not fantasy", *Quillette* 2 Feb. 2020 (www.quillette.com/2020/02/02/i-may-have-gender-dysphoria-but-i-still-prefer-to-base-my-life-on-biology-not-fantasy/) (accessed 2 Feb. 2020).

[4] Brendan O'Neill, "The witch hunt of JK Rowling", *Spiked* 20 Dec. 2019 (www.spiked-online.com/2019/12/20/the-witch-hunting-of-jk-rowling/) (accessed 30 Dec. 2019).

[5] Glynn Harrison, *A Better Story* (IVP UK, 2017), p 173.

4. Loud Power Versus Voiceless Victims

In 2020, Australian Catholic Cardinal, George Pell, walked free from prison after more than 400 days' incarceration over his conviction for historic sexual-abuse charges in 2018. The responses were as polarised as when he had walked into prison.

While this was first and foremost a criminal case, it soon became another skirmish in the ongoing cultural war, threatening at times to overshadow the actual search for justice. At times it was unedifying. Sides were chosen, and truth seemed to become less important than which side of the cultural narrative would prevail. Hence there was both great glee and great outrage when he walked free.

Pell had been the third most senior figure in the Vatican, tasked with sorting out the Holy City's financial scandals.

He had himself then been brought down by scandal, becoming the highest-profile churchman to be convicted of such crimes. Yet just over a year later the guilty verdict was unanimously overturned by the High Court in Australia in an appeal.

As Pell had been led from the dock just after initially being sentenced, there were shouts of joy and rapturous applause from those outside the court who viewed his conviction as a turning point in a long history of abuse by the Roman Catholic Church: abuse that had been aided and abetted by those within the church and other religious institutions.

The relief had been mingled with a sense of disbelief. Could it really be that one of the most powerful religious figures in the world was not above the law? Was the evidence of one nameless victim enough to conquer such a power disparity? The very issue—sex—that the church and Christianity had been scolding the secular world about for so long had now brought down a cardinal. Oh, the delicious irony!

It had felt like a turning point for many others too. Not everyone was cheering. Many, in Australia and beyond, were convinced that Pell was convicted upon scant, even unbelievable evidence. There was shock and anger, news articles claiming a witch hunt, social media outrage, and general confusion. Pell's conviction was simply proof that Christianity had become the whipping boy of Western culture. It was a show trial.

Those were the two extreme positions. There were many people in the middle. Many people who admitted they couldn't possibly know if Pell were guilty or not. These were historic crimes, where memories and recollections may have been flawed. But a jury of his peers had unanimously convicted him. Shouldn't we trust the process?

Yet the same legal processes just over a year later quashed the conviction. The decision by the High Court to overturn the case was either a result of power and influence at work in shady ways or proof that our legal system works. Whichever, you can be sure that it left people as divided as they had been when Pell was convicted.

Power Play or Victimhood?

Whatever position one takes regarding Cardinal Pell, the initial conviction exposed two cultural narratives that are in a death grip with each other in the West. Two narratives that are each incompatible with, or unwilling to co-exist with, the other. And, ironically, both are laying claims to victimhood.

The first narrative is about how the secular culture is riding roughshod over believers and church institutions, relegating them to the margins. This narrative tells Christians that they are right to feel hurt by the changes in popular assumptions about what leads to human flourishing, and urges them to fight back in whatever way they can. The second narrative comes from the secular point of view and is about the abuse of power which has led to trauma for so many people: from the covering up of sex scandals to the active repression of homosexuals, single mothers and other vulnerable groups.

Who is the victim here? Let me say from the outset that the victim narrative is a dangerous game for Christians to play—one that may have an initial sugar rush but risks becoming a bitter game indeed. While we may occasionally be victimised for being Christians in the West, we must resist the current temptation to find our worth or standing in actual or perceived victimhood.

We may feel that to allow our opponents to claim victimhood and not to highlight cases of our own is like fighting with one hand tied behind our backs. However, to begin with, we must acknowledge the very real and painful injustices that many minorities have experienced at the hands of a dominant culture. There have been victims, and the church must recognise that it has a special calling to the marginalised.

Yet, without taking away from these horrific situations, there is an impersonal identity-politics agenda that (ironically) views humans in a binary manner. You're either a victim or a perpetrator, says intersectionality ideology— and who wants to be a perpetrator, right? Individuals are encouraged to capitalise on an identity of victimhood to protect themselves from cultural criticism. New victim groupings are identified on a regular basis and people are rushing to sign up and make "victim" their primary identity.

Those who play at the card table of identity politics constantly search for the trump card that will grant them an elevated victim status and therefore place them beyond criticism by others, ushering in privileges hitherto held from them. Christians should not play this game. It gives us a losing hand, since other levels of victimhood are seen to have a stronger claim on the chips in the middle of the table. More importantly, it is not a tactic worthy of those whose identity and worth is in Christ.

Meanwhile, theologian Robyn Whitaker, writing in the progressive journal *The Conversation*, dismisses the idea of Christian victimhood outright:

"Let us be clear: Christians in Australia are not being persecuted. They have the freedom to gather and worship freely, to meet in public places, to join the army, to teach, to vote, and to be prime minister. Christians own and run vast institutions. They are still the largest religious affiliation in the country (at 52% in the 2016 census). These are hardly the signs of a persecuted group."[1]

And if that's the case in Australia, it is also true of other Western nations. In Britain, there are currently 26 Anglican bishops sitting in the unelected second chamber of Parliament, the House of Lords. And when every president in the US is either affiliated with a church denomination or is keen to be seen outside a church waving a Bible, then it's clear that we're a long way off from having to meet secretly in the catacombs.

The Contested Victim Narrative

Nevertheless, the conviction that Christianity is an increasingly powerless victim is one that has occupied the minds, books and blogs of many a Christian over the past two decades. It is believed that there is a concerted campaign by powerful figures who hate Christianity to marginalise and silence Christians. The secular framework in the West, so this story goes, is hostile to Christianity and has a vested interest in its decline. Christianity is subject to a new and unsavoury secular ideology. Stories abound of Christians being silenced in the workplace or refused positions on university courses for holding to a Christian sexual ethic. At the same time, every other belief system, regardless of its historicity or plausibility, along with all sorts of sexual practices that were barely mentionable just a few years ago, is now not only given free rein but celebrated.

Christians are being oppressed and hounded out of societal life, refused a place in the very public square that they helped to create. Think, for example, of tennis heroine Margaret Court, a 24 Grand Slam winner, whose public opposition to same-sex marriage has led to a campaign, led by fellow tennis greats Billie Jean King and Martina Navratilova, to have her name removed from the Margaret Court Arena, where the Australian Tennis Open is played each year.

Behind this strong anti-Christian push is a determination to relegate the foundational story of the West to the margins. Even now this is having dire consequences, since it is the Christian belief system that has both given and continues to uphold the modern human rights that the West takes for granted.

Yet despite these facts, Whitaker does have a point. We must admit that we are nowhere near having our throats slit on a lonely beach by anti-Christian terror groups, much less being refused employment in government departments on a grand scale by an act of Parliament, as many religious minorities experience around the world.

The other narrative states that, rather than being the victim, the church has been a power-abuser, and a powerful one, for too long. It is now experiencing its comeuppance. The progressive secular world is sloughing off its malign influence, leading us on to a brighter future devoid of dogma.

Christianity, so long aligned with the powerful and influential, can no longer assume a seat at the table. The balance is finally shifting, and Christianity—of whatever stripe—cannot simply dial the room service and have political, legal or cultural favours delivered on demand. When I saw the Academy Award-winning movie *Spotlight*, which is based on the *Boston Globe*'s investigation into historic child sexual abuses by Catholic priests in that city, I could not but be dismayed at how the church leveraged its political and legal influence to avoid justice. It's no surprise that so many have rejoiced to see the playing field being levelled. And, they say, if someone as powerful as Cardinal Pell had to be taken down in order to level it, then so be it.

The more thoughtful social commentators acknowledged that the message the church was supposed to be preaching centred on the crucified Christ, the ultimate story of weakness and the relinquishing of power. Yet, they pointed out, Christianity had repeatedly betrayed the weak and powerless: the church had first gained power and then abused it for centuries. Talk about not practising what you preach! In this telling of the story, the church is the biggest hypocrite around.

But, so the narrative goes, the tide is turning. Power is being transferred to the previously powerless. The secular authorities are finally giving a voice to those previously silenced. And the church is deservedly losing its voice and its position.

It's Complex

So, which narrative is true? Is the church a proud and powerful institution, aligning itself to whoever holds the purse strings and influence, silencing its victims and critics with power and legal threats? Or are Christians in the West now being marginalised, a persecuted and sidelined minority, increasingly refused a voice in the public square?

Well, as the little girl in the Old El Paso advertisement asks as her family vexes over choosing soft or hard taco shells,

"Why can't it be both?" Has the church been aligned to power too closely, ignoring the very voices that Jesus himself would have listened to? For sure. That seems beyond doubt. The Bible is vociferous against the sinful tendency of God's people to align themselves to power and to oppress the weak. A cursory reading of the Old Testament prophets, enforced by the words and actions of Jesus himself, proves this. No hard secularist speaks more harshly against the abuses of the church than the Founder of the church himself in Revelation 1 – 3.

But have Christians experienced an almost rabid hostility from an implacable secularism bent on removing their voices from the public square? This too seems obvious. There are organisations such as Humanists Australia, whose sole purpose is to achieve this shutdown by advocating the removal of faith-based chaplains in public schools and the end to Scripture lessons in classrooms. Such groups express glee when Christian groups are silenced on university campuses or have funding cut for their refusal to sign off on abortion.

Meanwhile public advocacy group American Atheists asserts that while 26 per cent of Americans are atheists, there is only one atheist in Congress. Their website promises the millions of Americans who stay at church simply for the sake of community that they can find a similar level of community if they leave church and join their association.[2]

I repeat, we should avoid the temptation to play the victim game. But whatever position you take, it seems indisputable that the church's role in our culture is shifting from central to marginal. That drift may take some time, for, as Tom Holland points out, the West is "firmly moored to its Christian past".[3] But those moorings will either slip off eventually, or be cut, and the Western ship will drift into uncharted waters. And they *are* uncharted. Australian foreign-affairs journalist and author, Greg Sheridan, asks:

"What will it mean for us when God is dead? Who, then, can humanity converse with, when we lose our oldest friend?"[4]

For all of secularism's self-confidence, we actually don't know what it will be like on the "other side of God". As Sheridan observes, taking the Christian frame for granted is a luxury only for those who have known no other frame. The cultural elimination of Christianity may well give way to a dry, arid post-Christian existence full of fear and empty of human kindness. Despite the secularist claims, there is no future devoid of dogma; there are only different types of dogmas. From the secular perspective, the Christianised culture we now have, featuring the fruit of the gospel, yet disconnected from the roots, could well be the best of a bad lot.

The Church as a Creative Minority

How should we move forward? How can Christians live in the knowledge that God is alive when everyone around considers him to be dead? Railing against the injustice of being sidelined is not proving to be an effective strategy.

Clamouring to retain our seat at the table is proving the law of diminishing returns. Perhaps it is time to embrace a place at the cultural margins. Perhaps, instead of railing against the injustices being done to us, we can concentrate on creating communities that are "thick and rich": communities that don't get caught up in the increasingly toxic culture war. We need a two-fold strategy to move forward. We must admit reality and then embrace possibility.

ADMIT REALITY

First, we should admit the reality of our failures. When we were not the minority grouping in the West, when we were not the powerless in the culture, when we were not having our voices shut down in the public square, we often failed to speak up for the voiceless, powerless minorities. Perhaps we spoke up for those who aligned with our values, but not for those who didn't. For many watching on, especially among those groups, it seems rich of us to demand better treatment than we meted out, now that the tables have been turned.

There are ways to repair this. Churches that have good track records at helping ethnic minorities—and others who have traditionally struggled to get a foothold—could be a great help to congregations who have previously ignored them. Similarly, a Christian friend of mine at the top end of town has joined a diversity committee to ensure that all minorities, faith groups, ethnic peoples, and sexual minorities are treated with equality and dignity.

questionable

Second, we should admit that we have a long way to go before we experience true hostility on a grand scale. Are we experiencing persecution or merely a persecution complex? The world is watching as we react to the pushback from hard secularism. And it simply isn't buying our persecution claim or our cries that we are the victims.

Bandying the "P" word about risks emptying it of meaning. Christians have been quick to call out the linguistic overreach of secularists who label biblical teaching on sexuality as homophobic or hate-speech. Let's not exacerbate the matter by using equally inflammatory language. Margaret Court condemned the move to rename the tennis arena as persecution, yet she pastors a large and well-financed church, is given a voice in the mainstream media on a regular basis, and sits court-side as a guest of Tennis Australia at any Australian Open match she chooses. These are hardly signs of someone who is being marginalised by the wider community.

Third, we must admit that the Bible tells us that whoever wants to live a godly life in Christ will be persecuted, and that those who do evil will increase (2 Timothy 3 v 12-13). This is not to adopt a defeatist attitude about where our culture is drifting but to know that the common experience of many Christians down the centuries has been one not of power but of persecution. What this persecution looks like varies from century to century and society to society, but we follow a crucified Messiah, so why expect less for ourselves? We may well find that certain work environments are closed to us, that universities refuse campus facilities to Christian groups, and that we risk our careers stalling by refusing to take part in Wear It Purple Day (a corporate initiative in Australia to celebrate the LGBTQI community). But if we cannot bear these inconveniences, we will be incensed or despairing should real and lasting persecution kick in.

EMBRACE POSSIBILITY

If admitting these realities seems negative, there is a flip side. This cultural shift is giving us the chance to embrace possibilities that spring from the cultural changes and challenges we are facing.

Christians should prepare themselves, emotionally and practically, to live as a community on the cultural margins—and to embrace this place. There is little to be gained and much to lose by following the rest of society down the culture-war rabbit hole.

Already the term "evangelical" is becoming a code word for right-wing warrior. I was headed home on an interstate flight recently, and the young man sitting next to me wanted to chat. As soon as he heard what I did for a living, he asked, "You're not one of those evangelicals, are you?" What he means by that word and what I mean by it are two different things, but there is a widespread perception that to be an evangelical today aligns you with right-wing politics, a harsh social agenda and an aggressive attitude towards migrants.

But our hope is not in winning a culture war. Our hope is in the One who has defeated our true enemies—Satan, sin and death—and who has given us his victory. We will waste a lot of emotional and actual energy if we don't cling to this truth.

Embracing the margins will take the heat out of the debate. We will no longer feel as if we're fighting for the centre in an all-or-nothing battle. For many Christians, Twitter and Facebook have become the means to push back hard against anti-Christian sentiment, whether from legal, political or cultural channels. How much time should we spend doing this? Is it all that helpful in the task of showcasing Jesus? Christians, of all people, should have no fear of being viewed as wrong. We are not self-justified people; we are Jesus-justified people.

Second, staying on the margins gives us a chance to observe the bigger picture and plan for what will inevitably happen when rampant individualism starts to bear bitter fruit. Even now, the hard-progressive side of the culture war is starting to show cracks. The sexual agenda it promotes is beginning to rack up a body count of those who have found it wanting, and of those who think untested secular theories are being pushed upon us too quickly. This has resulted in a strange paradox: our culture has rarely been

more hostile towards the gospel, but at the same time it has rarely been more open either. University Christian groups in Australia have anecdotally reported some of their most fruitful gospel years recently, as students arrive on campus with almost zero frameworks for navigating an increasingly complex culture.

Our time would be better spent preparing for what I believe will be a tsunami of the broken and wounded who wash up on our shores. Author Dale Kuehne observes:

"Despite its triumph, the iWorld is not perfect. Two of the primary difficulties facing people in the iWorld are loneliness and insecurity. These are inherent by-products of individualism. If individual freedom is the goal and the means of achieving this freedom is replacing relationships of obligation and responsibility with a world of relational choice, then a certain amount of loneliness and insecurity will result."[5]

And that "certain amount" is, in places, reaching a tipping point. A friend who works in a Christian organisation which conducts workshops in public high schools told me that there are three questions consistently asked of her by young people. They centre around lack of meaning and purpose, loss of identity and the risk of never being forgiven.

Are we ready in our churches for that cohort to reach adulthood and arrive on our doorsteps—uncertain and confused and looking for meaningful answers? Have we set aside enough time, and shaped our own understanding of meaning, identity and forgiveness around the gospel deeply enough, to be prepared for what could be a wonderful gospel harvest? We can refuse the language of victimhood because to do so allows us to make the most of the evangelistic opportunities that will come our way.

When the actual victims of the culture start looking for grace and solace from its bruising brutality, we should make it easy for them to conclude that we have been the ones to provide that all along.

There are many other possibilities that embracing the cultural margin will give us, and we will explore these in the final section of this book. But for now, let's decide not to be afraid. When the Lord assures Paul that "my grace is sufficient for you, for my power is made perfect in weakness" (2 Corinthians 12 v 9), he is not pulling a pastoral rabbit out of a theological hat. Power made perfect in weakness has been God's way all along. He chose Israel because of his love, not their impressiveness. He whittled away Gideon's army so that no one would be under any illusions about who won the battle and how. He sent Jesus to die on the cross, looking weak and powerless to all the world—but not to God. Let's therefore hold on to the paradoxical conviction that to allow ourselves to be weak might actually be where our strength lies.

Endnotes

[1] Robyn Whitaker, "Christians in Australia are not persecuted, and it is insulting to argue they are", *The Conversation*, 30 May 2018 (www.theconversation.com/christians-in-australia-are-not-persecuted-and-it-is-insulting-to-argue-they-are-96351) (accessed: 29 Jan. 2020).

[2] www.atheists.org.

[3] *Dominion*, p 9-10.

[4] Greg Sheridan, *God Is Good For You* (Allen and Unwin, 2018), p 1.

[5] *Sex and the iWorld*, p 77.

5. Self-Denial Versus Self-Actualisation

When British TV personality Phillip Schofield came out live on the UK morning show he co-hosts, there was an outpouring of affirmation and congratulations. Schofield, for so long the familiar, safe face of daytime TV, made the emotional announcement in early February 2020. He spoke on Instagram of the pain it had caused his family, but also of his relief: "Every day on *This Morning* I sit in awe of those who have been brave and open in confronting their truth—so now it's time for me to share mine."

Schofield's wife, Steph, and their two daughters watched as he came out on live television in front of the rest of Britain. By Schofield's own admission in media interviews afterwards, it has been a difficult time for his spouse of 27 years and his twenty-something daughters. He also confessed that he did not know if his marriage would survive, and refused to say if he was in a relationship with another man.

Such "comings out" are painful. Schofield is one of a rare breed who gets to do it on national television. And he has not been flippant about it—he acknowledges the hurt and conflict, especially for his family, whom he evidently loves.

Yet it is the response to Schofield's conviction that he had to be honest with himself that is most revealing.

Comedian David Walliams tweeted, "I am sending all my love to Phillip Schofield today. I have always held him in the highest regard, and now have nothing but respect and admiration for him." Celebrity lifestyle guru Gok Wan praised him for his "bravery". And *Dancing on Ice* judge John Barrowman tweeted this about the show's host: "So proud of you and your family Phillip. Welcome to your true and authentic self."

This final comment summarises the general response in the media. Schofield is now being his "authentic self"; he knew since before he was married that he was gay but suppressed it. As this narrative goes, his life up to this point was therefore less than authentic. His wedding vows, his marriage, the heterosexual family man: this other Phillip Schofield was the inauthentic version, untrue to himself, and in the process, untrue to the long line of those who have shown their own authenticity by coming out. He was late to be brave and "do the right thing", but he has now put this right.

This issue is bigger than Phillip Schofield, or even his family. It is about what it means to be authentic in our culture. Coming out, especially for those previously living in heterosexual relationships, hits the authenticity jackpot. Meanwhile, the flip side—moving from open homosexuality to celibacy or, worse, heterosexuality—is viewed as inauthentic at the extreme. Rejecting your "true self" is to do violence not only to yourself but to a wider cause.

Self-Authenticity

There is another layer to this. Authenticity is a solo game. In our culture, being true to oneself is the goal of life—the pathway to happiness. This mantra is never challenged, let alone held up to scrutiny. Any idea that Schofield might *refuse* to come out or might put his desires second for the sake of being true to his marriage and family is not in play. It would be an inauthentic act, given the *a priori* conviction that self-fulfilment is our highest good.

Such a view would sound strange—indeed, almost incomprehensible—to someone from, say, eastern Africa, where individual desires are subordinated to social, religious and family commitments, and authenticity is about fulfilling one's duty to one's community. Missionary friends among Mozambique's Yao people report how even walking alone is not a thing there. When I asked how an introvert could exist within such a culture, I was told that if you are walking along the road in a group, you don't have to speak, and people will respect that; but the thought that you would walk alone would not cross even the most introverted mind.

You prove yourself false in Mozambique by taking isolated decisions. This is illustrated by the implications for evangelism there: the Islamic faith of the Yao is not the spiritual choice of *individuals*, but the assumed belief of a *people*. To be Yao is to be Muslim. Changing religions is a category error and a risk to community cohesion.

Even in the West, such community bonding was evident until quite recently. Christianity, rooted in less transient communities than we have now, assumed that self-denial, not self-expression, was the path to social cohesion and the common good. To refuse self-denial was to refuse true life.

Why am I making much of this? Because we too— Christians who sign off on the creeds, recite the prayers of confession, and share communion and the occasional lunch—are steeped in the individualistic narrative of the authentic self. Sermon series titles based around individual happiness and self-flourishing reveal that swathes of the church have fallen for the authenticity hoax.

I recently watched the Julie Andrews classic *The Sound of Music* (for research purposes, of course). When the abbess starts singing to an unhappy and uncertain Maria about what she should do, most viewers don't even blink. We never question that the leader of a cloistered order, "married to Christ", in pre-war Europe would suggest that the path to true life is to:

Climb every mountain
Ford every stream
Follow every rainbow
Till you find your dream:

A dream that will need
All the love you can give
Every day of your life
For as long as you live.

Of course the abbess should say that. Why wouldn't she? Here's why not: because the Christian faith is not simply concerned with finding love in this life, or indeed with finding anything in this life. It is about finding life after this life ends. That's what a real-life abbess would say. *The Sound of Music* is a Hollywood movie marinated in the "self-fulfilment now" narrative that Tinseltown has been producing for a century.

Your Best Life Now?

This glittery view of what life is about, and its co-opting of a religious order, directly contrasts with Jesus' words in Matthew 16 v 24-25:

> *Whoever wants to be my disciple must deny themselves and take up their cross and follow me. For whoever wants to save their life will lose it, but whoever loses their life for me will find it.*

Self-denial: it's not just in the small print. Jesus is explicit that self-denial, not self-fulfilment, is the path to life. He calls his disciples to make the costly decision to take up their cross and die to themselves in exchange for the finding and saving of their lives. There is great reward in self-denial. It's just not now. Or at least it is not fully now.

Jesus also warns that those who seek their own safety now will lose their lives in the long run. But why? What is so bad about self-fulfilment that it could be fatal?

Self-fulfilment promises "your best life now!" It shares self-denial's goal: life. But self-fulfilment is intent on getting its reward now—and will play whatever game necessary to do so. This desire to get now what Jesus promises later is the source of sin—a rejection of God and his plan for the world. That's why it leads to destruction. Adam and Eve's problem was not so much the desire to have a knowledge of good and evil but their refusal to trust God's words for it. They fast-tracked the process, or so they thought. That was the disobedience.

This is a pattern we see throughout the Bible. In 1 Samuel 13 King Saul is reprimanded because he disobeys the command to wait for Samuel to arrive before offering the sacrifice. Why does he not wait? He fears the disapproval of his troops now, rather than seeking the approval of God later when Samuel turns up.

Self-denial, on the other hand, calls us to lean on God and trust his words, refusing the deadly path that Adam and Eve took and accepting God's vision for flourishing rather than constructing our own. And it calls us to do that even when it means losing out now in the hope of life later.

In the Sermon on the Mount, Jesus promised that eternity belonged to those who are meek now, who mourn now and who are pure in heart now. And membership of that group is not guaranteed by membership of an evangelical church. In Jesus' day, many religious people did believe in him but would not publicly confess him: "They loved human praise more than praise from God" (John 12 v 43). That warns us of the possibility that today's religious people—the most cast-iron of evangelical churches, for example, that proclaim self-denial and preach against the prosperity gospel—could be equally susceptible to believing the "best life now" project.

The two things we fear losing the most are certainty and comfort. As Christians we have taken these for granted (as has the rest of our culture), even though we would affirm that our one comfort in life and death is that we are not our own. Until, of course, a global pandemic hits and someone buys up all the toilet paper. Our reactions show where our comfort lies! It's easy to craft a life in which our desire for self-fulfilment lies unnoticed until challenged.

There are myriad self-fulfilment struggles we deal with as Christians, without the word "sex" even being raised. What about our right to be right, *now*? That attitude has destroyed many congregations who can sign off on the tightest credal statement. Bitterness and unforgiveness have torn some evangelical churches apart. Getting what we want *now* seems preferable to the implicit answer to Paul's question: "Why not rather be wronged?"

(1 Corinthians 6 v 7). Is Paul content with injustice? No! But this is a call to wait for God's justice: a call to deny the self now in order to gain life later.

Or what about when a financially or relationally costly decision that could bear much gospel fruit in the future is rejected by our church on the basis that it puts us out *now*? We can get on with ministry the way we want to— yet even if it's the "orthodox" way, it could still be self-fulfilment masquerading as prudence.

The other viral crisis in recent years has been the absence of humble, godly church leadership. Many harsh shepherds have promoted self-interest and personal agendas at the cost of the sheep. This too is simply another way to circumvent self-denial for the sake of self-fulfilment. It's never put like that, of course; which simply makes self-fulfilment more difficult to root out.

This seemingly sanctified self-fulfilment agenda has left us unprepared now that the sexual agenda has arrived on the church's shores. If we haven't pumped self-denial iron in "spiritual" matters, then we won't in sexual matters. If our reflex has become self-fulfilment, we'll employ therapeutic language instead of more challenging biblical descriptions. We will label as "brave", "being true to yourself" and "leaving bigotry behind" what the Bible calls "falling away" (Hebrews 3 v 12, ESV), being "in love with this present age" (2 Timothy 4 v 10, ESV)—or the graphic, and somewhat stomach-churning, description of a sow that has been cleaned now returning to the mud (2 Peter 2 v 22).

We must say no to both secular and sacred self-fulfilment agendas, and contest any vision of the good life that is grounded in self-fulfilment and self-expression rather than self-denial. The gospel *will* lead to human flourishing; but it has a different understanding of how to achieve such flourishing.

The truth is, the historical events *The Sound of Music* depicts were too bracing and challenging for Hollywood to countenance. Maria did not marry Georg von Trapp because she was in love with him. As she recounted in *The Story of the Trapp Family Singers*, she fell in love with the children at first sight, not their father. When he asked her to marry him, she was not sure if she should abandon her religious calling but was advised by the nuns to marry Georg:

> *"I really and truly was not in love. I liked him but didn't love him. However, I loved the children, so in a way I really married the children ... by and by I learned to love him more than I have ever loved before or after."*[1]

Self-denial did indeed usher in life.

Authentic Authenticity

All of this is complicated by the paradox that authenticity is our highest cultural currency only if it can pass the sniff test of conspicuous outward self-denial. Authenticity pronouncements cannot be seen to be self-serving. Self-fulfilment must have a veneer of self-denial, or it will be kicked to the kerb.

This has been highlighted, brutally, for actor Jameela Jamil, star of the NBC sitcom *The Good Place*. Jamil came out as queer shortly after Schofield's announcement. She had been suffering criticism for accepting a role as a TV judge on an HBO voguing competition—a style of dance that originated with African American and Latino queer people in Harlem, New York. The problem was, Jamil was neither African American nor part of the queer community. When she came out, her announcement was met with derision from some quarters and hostile silence from others. Why? It failed the conspicuous self-denial test.

Queer author Amelia Abraham said of Jamil:

"Her coming out feels inauthentic to people. It feels she was on the back foot, or reactionary, or the timing was off because it came just after she was criticised for being a judge on a voguing show."[2]

 Paradoxically, coming out has to look like self-denial to be considered authentic. For Schofield, 57 years of age and married, the revelation seems costly. This is why he has been lauded as "brave". But for Jamil, coming out seemed like a handy ticket to get out of a tight spot. There was no risk—only gain. Now, ironically, she is paying for it.

Christians can also mask their self-promotion as self-denial. We proudly Instagram the number of reps in our Crossfit session, or put the 35km run we did on Strava (guilty, Your Honour), or publicise the hours of study we put in to achieve the grades that would get us into the course we wanted at university. Yet the test comes if we are asked to give up Crossfit because our prayer life has fallen away; or if we are injured when running and have to do rehab for six months and still be godly in our attitudes (also guilty, Your Honour); or if we are asked to meet one-on-one with a new Christian and risk missing that final one percent in the exam. Is our self-denial actual self-denial or merely a deliberately conspicuous veneer, designed—whether we admit it to ourselves or not—to mask selfishness?

This is why it's helpful to define "authentic" authenticity, so to speak—and this is why we look to Jesus. Jesus was the most authentic person ever. He was concerned not for his individual good but for the good of the *community* around him. He put aside his rights *now* for the sake of glory *later*. He rejected any *hypocritical* veneer and displayed *genuine* godliness and humility. It is a tragic irony that by rejecting Jesus' call to authenticity, we will forfeit the life that Jesus offers.

Who Wins?

Both authenticity calls cannot be true. One must be proved false. Yet when and how? On the surface it seems the world is winning. Schofield's coming out is the moment in which he truly begins to live. Who would dare challenge this narrative? That would be heartlessness, surely. Worse, according to this script, it would heighten the chance of suicide among those struggling with their sexual identity.

No public narrative exists in which Schofield's authenticity would be displayed by him prioritising his wife's desires instead of his own. Gok Wan issued no tweet praising her. John Barrowman would be nonplussed if she said her true and authentic self was found in her marriage.

There is a grimacing skull lurking behind the culture's wide, authentic smile. Death, not life, lies there. It is ironic, but inevitable, that the cultural story cannot be fully authentic in its authenticity. Inconvenient truths must be hidden if this cultural story is to trump other gospels.

Walt Heyer, an American man who was encouraged by a top gender specialist to become female due to his gender dysphoria, discovered this to his cost. Told that his problems would be resolved by becoming female, he endured 13 years of physical and psychological trauma before he transitioned back and started to deal with underlying issues of childhood sexual abuse. He now runs a support network for those who regret their transition, and he challenges the media's refusal to acknowledge this community as one which is damaged, and also growing.[3]

Meanwhile, an Australian report has claimed that there is no evidence to show that the suicide rate of transitioners is any lower than among those who haven't transitioned.[4] Several European governments, busy prepping to introduce legislation to lower the age limit for transitioning therapies, have got cold feet as medical misgivings come to the surface.

Yet let's not simply view this through the lens of the increasingly toxic culture wars. This is as much about individuals as it is about ideology. The quest for authenticity is real and heartfelt. The desire for some fixed reference point that makes sense of who I am and where I am headed is a genuine *cri de coeur*.

Christians believe that human hearts are restless until they find their rest in God. We were made for meaning and purpose: to discover our given identity. The church— and the gospel story it narrates and embodies—is well placed, therefore, to offer cultural refugees some hope in the midst of a failing self-fulfilment story.

Insecurity, depression and anxiety abound, despite the time, money and effort being spent on discovering our authentic selves. And if the cracks are appearing within the cultural story at the top of the pyramid, then those cracks are veritable chasms further down. Part of the reason we experience hostility when we offer self-denial as the path to life is precisely because the cracks are there. They are busily being papered over by those who have no interest in us pointing them out.

This is not to say that the self-fulfilment authenticity narrative is an unmitigated disaster. It seems to be working out just fine for many people, especially those with the finances and influence make it, at least in part, work for them. But if we take Jesus at his word, the ultimate conclusion is death. And if the destination is death, then there will be hints along the way that that is the endpoint. Those hints—that transitioning does not bring fulfilment and that building your own identity does not bring happiness—are becoming clearer to those with eyes to see. And increasingly those eyes belong to desperate people who have searched everywhere for self-fulfilment, yet have come up empty.

Happily, the path of self-denial that leads to life shows clear signs of that life along the way. And why would it not, since Jesus walked it first? Everywhere Jesus went, true life followed. Jesus was the most authentic person ever: the most honest, the bravest, the most admirable. It makes sense that the life of the cross and of self-denial will contain a sweetness and lightness that confound those who reject its central tenets.

Sex is not the only issue—and not even the most important one—for which this is true. As I mentioned in the Introduction, this book deals with sexuality a lot not because I am obsessed with it (an accusation often levelled at orthodox Christians) but because the culture is. Western culture is obsessed with sexuality because it has declared that our deepest, truest, most authentic self is discovered there. Yet we say otherwise. It is as the church is seen to live the self-denying life in all areas (including but not limited to sexuality) that we signal, even to those still trying to find their true self in gender and sexual expression, that there is something about being part of the people of God that is winsome and true and lifegiving.

When we show undeserved forgiveness in "cancel culture", in which every indiscretion—past or present—is pounced upon, and in which careers and friendships are ended because of a tweet; when we show costly generosity in a greedy culture; when we fail to take advantage of people in an every-person-for-themselves culture; when we esteem others as greater than ourselves in a self-promoting culture—we are sending powerful signals to those who would otherwise reject us for our views on sex.

It's first of all confusing ("How can they be so loving when they reject the idea that love is love?"); then it's intriguing ("I don't agree with how intolerant they are supposed to be, but they welcomed me in"); next, it's attractive ("It looks and feels and sounds better than what I'm currently doing"); and finally, it's compelling ("I think that this might just be where true life is found").

Confusing, intriguing, attractive, compelling. Can our Christian communities be these things to those who are desperately seeking their authentic selves? Can our churches become the mile-markers for those on a journey seeking the pathway to life? Can they keep us from straying from that pathway? Jesus bids us follow that narrow road, because the alternative is a broad way that leads to destruction. With that in mind, we turn in the next section to a credible map that will help those seeking life to find it in Jesus, and to see it exhibited by his followers.

Endnotes

[1] Maria Augusta Trapp, *The Story of the Trapp Family Singers* (William Morrow Paperbacks, 2001: first published 1957).

[2] Nosheen Iqbal, "Phillip Schofield and Jameela: two tales of coming out", *The Guardian*, 9 Feb. 2020 (www.theguardian.com/society/2020/feb/08/phillip-schofield-and-jameela-jamil-two-tales-of-coming-out) (accessed 5 Mar. 2020).

[3] Walt Heyer, "Hormones, surgery, regret: I was a transgender woman for 8 years—time I can't get back", *USA Today*, 11 Feb. 2019 (www.usatoday.com/story/opinion/voices/2019/02/11/transgender-debate-transitioning-sex-gender-column/1894076002/) (accessed 18 Mar. 2020).

[4] Bernard Lane, "Gender clinics operate with weak evidence, most doctors unaware", *The Australian*, 5 Mar. 2020 (www.theaustralian.com.au/nation/gender-clinics-operate-with-weak-evidence-most-doctors-unaware/news-story/8cc1aae227a909231be52b124223016e) (accessed 6 Mar. 2020).

6. Don't Renovate the Wrong House

(A Strategy for Church)

"**W**e no longer hold the cultural reins. Our views are not respected. Once we were thought of as fairly harmless (if we were thought of at all). Now we are seen as part of the problem in society—a group intent on holding things back. Once we were considered important in the government's scheme. Now we are viewed by the government as an impediment to its vision of a flourishing future. Once we were allowed to get on with our specific worship practices. Now these same practices are viewed with hostility and deep suspicion by our neighbours, who are more than happy to inform on us. Identifying as the people of God is on the back burner now. The cultural heat has been turned up. Better to keep our heads down and wait for the angry cultural storm to pass."

Sound familiar? Actually, I'm not talking about the present day. Welcome to the world of Haggai. This was the lament of the Jewish people after exile. Their world had changed beyond recognition. Returning from Babylon, they began to re-establish their identity, rebuilding Jerusalem and laying the foundations of the new temple on the rubble of the old. (At this point, if you have time, why not give Haggai a quick read? It's only two chapters.)

Here's what we find: Israel had run out of steam. God's people were flagging in the face of a harsh post-exile reality. God had previously given them an identity at Mount Sinai:

Now if you obey me fully and keep my covenant, then out of all nations you will be my treasured possession. Although the whole earth is mine, you will be for me a kingdom of priests and a holy nation. (Exodus 19 v 5-6)

But surely things had changed too much for this identity to remain intact?

A Loss of Identity

After all: what kingdom? They had no God-anointed king, just a governor appointed by Persia. Treasured possession of God? Their neighbours were hostile, stymying their efforts to rebuild. Kingdom of priests and holy nation? Work on the temple of the Lord, the place where sacrifices for sin were made and God had chosen to dwell, had ceased. The covenant promises were a distant memory. And now, with economic woes setting in, the best strategy seemed to be to get on with normal life and not make a fuss. Bunker down. Fit in. After all, it was working for the other nations.

The straw that broke the camel's back for Israel was the unfavourable report from those very nations, who wrote to the king of Babylon to accuse the Jews of stirring up rebellion by rebuilding the temple. The king's reply to these officials is telling:

> *Now issue an order to these men to stop work, so that this city will not be rebuilt until I so order. Be careful not to neglect this matter. Why let this threat grow, to the detriment of the royal interests? (Ezra 4 v 21-22)*

The Jews were the bad guys, the flies in the ointment of human flourishing. Their interests were on a collision course with those of their Persian rulers. Something had to give. As the dust settled on the building site, it settled on God's people too. They settled into a quieter life and adopted a less God-focused identity—one that would not upset the empire's cultural and social building program. And not only did they settle into this identity, they justified it:

> *These people say, "The time has not yet come to rebuild the LORD's house." (Haggai 1 v 2)*

God's people had convinced themselves that their inaction was strategic. *The time will come, for sure, when we raise our heads above the cultural parapet, but it's not yet. Now it's time to keep our heads down.*

Yet amid this spiritual inertia, they were busy nonetheless. God says:

Is it a time for you yourselves to be living in your panelled houses, while this house remains a ruin? (Haggai 1 v 4)

He accuses the people of each being "busy with [their] own house" (v 9). Israel is still in the house-building game—it's just that it's their own houses they're focusing on, and "panelled houses" at that. Ouch! God has visited the covenant curses upon them, withering their crops and reducing their economy to bring them back to living for him. But they've still got just enough resources to forge this other identity—one that fits better with the interests of the pagan king. And they justify it on the basis that "the time has not yet come".

A Loss of God's Glory

God does not see this as a strategic decision. He sees it as a sinful decision—one that robs him of glory. The word "glory" is constantly used in the Bible. It means the weightiness of something or someone, or their worthiness to garner our time and attention. We give glory or honour to what we consider worthy of it. The constant question is, does the object of our honour qualify for the level of honour we are giving it? Will it hold the weight of our glory?

Something with "little" intrinsic glory is less worthy of our worship. Something—or someone—with "great" glory is more worthy of it. And that's the constant battle in Scripture. Where will humans direct glory and honour? Haggai says the people of God have made a poor choice:

> *This is what the LORD Almighty says: "Give careful thought to your ways. Go up into the mountains and bring down timber and build my house, so that I may take pleasure in it and be honoured," says the LORD. (Haggai 1 v 7-8)*

It is time to change their ways and to honour God. After all, if glory is not being directed towards God, it is being directed somewhere else.

It's not just Israel: it's all of us. We were wired to worship—created to give glory. The late American author David Foster Wallace delivered the commencement address at Kenyon College, a US liberal arts institute, in 2005. His speech, which is essential listening, cuts to the heart of the human condition:

> *"In the day-to-day trenches of adult life, there is actually no such thing as atheism. There is no such thing as not worshipping. Everybody worships. The only choice we get is what to worship."[1]*

He lists a variety of gods (and goddesses) that one could worship. But he gets to the heart of the issue when he exposes the folly of worshipping—or giving glory to—things that will not hold worship's weight:

> *"Anything else you worship will eat you alive. If you worship money and things, if they are where you tap real meaning in life, then you will never have enough, never feel you have enough.*

It's the truth. Worship your body and beauty and sexual allure and you will always feel ugly. And when time and age start showing, you will die a million deaths before they finally grieve you."

Foster Wallace nailed the worship problem better than most pastors! But I wonder, how many of those who sat in that assembly are now not only worshipping those very things but—as today's advertising executives, PR consultants, journalists, online media influencers and movie directors—are also using their gifts and talents to encourage us to as well?

A Blueprint for Rebuilding

The call to honour God in the face of cultural hostility and beguiling identity-shaping alternatives is still our call today. The personal building projects, in which "Persian kings" stare down our temple-building efforts while encouraging us to focus on our panelled houses, must be resisted. What does that look like for us, two and a half millennia after Haggai's time? What follows is a blueprint for us in the 21st century.

PREFERENCE GOD'S PEOPLE

If we look back in 30 years' time and ask what basic strategy has been most successful in staying the hand of secular culture, I'm convinced that the sheer simplicity of committing to meet with God's people will win hands down. The church is the New Testament temple of God, and we neglect this building program at our peril.

Preferencing God's people is a simple strategy, yet it is often beyond us. We live in a time when everyone is rushing off to their own panelled houses and personal improvement projects. Modern life, with its virtual technologies and physical mobility, enables and encourages this. And Christians are not immune.

Expressive individualism says, "You do you". It does not countenance sacrificing self for the sake of others, especially those outside immediate family or friendship groups. When we read memes saying we should cut the negative people out of our lives, we find it easy to justify curating a circle of acquaintances who confirm our biases and never challenge us, and whose lifestyles or circumstances fit perfectly with our own.

We must learn to do the opposite. If Jesus had cut the negative people out of his life, he would have been left by himself. Instead he went to the cross for the sake of exactly those people. That's the level of commitment we are to give to one another. We are to cultivate Christian communities in which our common characteristic is Jesus. A sure-fire apologetic for the church is its ability to create deep community across social and cultural boundaries. As Western cultures fracture into toxic tribalism, it's crucial for churches to form deep, thick communities, based around more than convenience.

This will cost us. Preferencing long-term church relationships may mean forgoing career advancement in another city because we are a crucial part of the body in our current church. It may mean sidelining relationships that merely reflect our own interests, for the sake of the weaker and more needy among us—those with whom, apart from Jesus, we have little in common. It may mean living in an area that we don't particularly like, simply because that's where God's people meet. These responses are deeply challenging to those of us whose reflex is to "rush off" to the panelled houses of our self-construction project.

Too often, there is as much churn in the church as in the world. People "upgrade" churches like they do cars—moving every four or five years. How can you build stable, honest and loving communities that offer significance, hope and forgiveness to a weary world, if you don't stay long enough yourself to see this happen? Don't be surprised if your children walk away from a people of faith to whom you yourself were barely committed—because their only long-term friendships are in the world.

We need to do life together—church services, meals, times of *ad hoc* gathering in which conversations are sprinkled with grace. That is what will challenge a culture in which it is taken for granted that creating a fantastic career edifice, building a trophy cabinet of holiday and lifestyle experiences, or spending time, energy and money on self-actualising projects are paramount.

This is not about keeping Christians busy. It is about first defining ourselves as the gathered people of God and then shaping our lives around that commitment. It will mean sharing meals with people when it's easier not to. Sharing more of your finances with those who have less. Sharing more of *you* when you're tired or grumpy.

Do not underestimate how attractive this is to outsiders. A friend I go running with, who is not a Christian, often talks about how she feels almost jealous of my church community. She and her husband are migrants in Australia and feel the lack of family. They look at our church and see a support network that feels like, looks like and operates like the family they don't have. My friend perceives something good in what we have, even as we ourselves allow familiarity to breed contempt.

PROCLAIM GOD'S PRAISES

The church must, secondly, rediscover its core practice of proclaiming the praises of God. If one thing refreshed me in the COVID-19 pandemic, it was how theologies that failed to challenge secular culture's primary identity markers (whether material, ideological or sexual) were sidelined. Amidst all the difficulties, I found there was a sweetness in Easter 2020 because the Lord Jesus, and the hope we have in him, was front and centre. It meant more than it had done before to know that to have Jesus and nothing else, even in the face of death, meant we had everything.

The pandemic swept the trivial aside, exposing the panelled houses of our unworthy worship. Formerly inspirational TED talks that were really little more than lifestyle chats, therapeutic programs or cultural and political pitches suddenly felt lame. People were dying, jobs were being shed; we were all in lockdown. Where was the hope in a self-improvement program? To know Jesus as our only hope is paramount.

Whatever the near future holds, churches that have neglected the deepest need of the Christian community—namely, to get to know Jesus better and to allow him to reshape our identity as the people of God—will eventually cave in to a hostile culture and follow the path of least resistance. We see this happening already in the area of sexual ethics. In three decades' time, churches that have not placed the proclamation of King Jesus front and centre will either be in decline or will have closed. We must not be swayed by hostility—after all, Jesus himself was more than familiar with it.

When Jesus and his goodness are proclaimed in our buildings, it will seep out into the rest of our lives. His name will be spoken around our dinner tables and even in our workplaces. He will be shown to be our hope—our very public hope—even as secular hostility rises. The world is happy to have spiritual belief as a privatised side dish. Let's encourage each other to reinvest our everyday language with "Jesus" talk, and to speak of him as if he matters in the "real world".

How Jesus-focused are you? Are your non-Christian friends convinced that you are more enthusiastic about Jesus than you are about your renovation project or the university grades of your children? Are they amazed by how much Jesus sets the tone of everything you do?

Being besotted with Jesus may bring scorn, but he is still our best asset! What if being seen as "the weirdo" is actually our strength?

Our desire, publicly at least, has often been to present Christianity as a sensible option among the other options offered by the world. Our strategy seems to have been that if we could state our case in such a way that people think we have the same goals and values as them, then we would succeeded in convincing them.

 But what we believe about Jesus is absolutely weird and often off-putting to the modern mind. It's also a direct challenge to its core values and practices. Most of the time, no one wants to know about sensible Christian views on global poverty. Everyone wants to know what we think about sexuality. We can only hold them off for so long with "sensible".

And why bother? There are thousands of lost, hurting and confused people who have been chewed up by the culture and are looking for something more: something different. Perhaps it is time for us to be more "angular" in the public square and lose the desire to be seen as sensible. Instead of falling back into a rather lame "Here's what we think would be good for society", let's present Jesus as the central reason for our convictions. That is what lost people need. We need to play up our differences as much as our similarities.

Without Jesus we have no compelling reason to offer any vision for human flourishing beyond what the world already has. Our arguments for a Christian social and sexual ethic sound to some like little more than a desire to regain power. But Jesus' resurrection ushered in a new ethic. Our hope for the culture is not the image of Adam and Eve in the garden but the image of Jesus in the new creation.

That's why, both personally and in community, we should make much of praising Jesus and focusing on what he has done for us. Sure, we can spend time planning and talking about what we can do for him—but those things can only spring from our awe and wonder at his grace for us. And then from letting that everyday praise make its way into our everyday conversation.

 If we are focused on Jesus, then we will not become self-entitled or embittered Christians who play the victim card and get angry when society pushes against us. We will instead be filled with joy. When we don't join in the cheers when our cultural enemies *lose* a battle, or when we don't shout angrily at them when they *win* a battle, it will only be because Jesus is our hope and joy—and he is our example of what it looks like to entrust yourself to the One who judges justly (1 Peter 2 v 23).

PROMOTE GOD'S PROMISES

It sometimes feels like we have little to offer the world, especially when it tells us to get on the right side of history. We can easily become dispirited and pull up the drawbridge to protect ourselves, as the progressive rainbow framework promises a future using the terms, images and ideas given to it by the historic Christian faith—a future that leaves us on the outside.

But ironically there's currently an openness to the gospel message in our society, despite the hostility. Historic levels of anxiety, fear and loneliness abound. The church is a community of promised resurrection hope in a society that is terrified of death and anxious about missing out on the good stuff that advertising offers. We have something which many in the world want but cannot find. It may not always feel as though this is true, but it is true nonetheless.

The people of God in Haggai's time listen to him. They rebuild the temple. And then God's words come to Zerubbabel, their leader:

Who of you is left who saw this house in its former glory? How does it look to you now? Does it not seem to you like nothing? (Haggai 2 v 3)

The glory of the temple doesn't feel true. It doesn't feel plausible. Everyone can see that the current rebuild looks rubbish. But the foundations of God's resurrection hope are being laid:

"The glory of this present house will be greater than the glory of the former house," says the LORD Almighty.
(Haggai 2 v 9)

That's the promise: future glory. For Zerubbabel, hope was found in looking forward to a temple filled with the glory of his descendant, King Jesus, who would stride into that very building hundreds of years later. And for us? Our hope is in that day when the resurrected and reigning Jesus returns.

The church is the temple of God, headed for a glory we cannot even imagine. For the moment, that description of the church may not feel true. It may not feel plausible. But because of God's future resurrection promise, it is. So we can serve a needy world in costly ways because we know the future! We can serve a world that scorns and rejects us; we can be known as those who add value to our communities through resources, volunteering, social concern, financial support and professional pro bono work, because we look to God's promises. Churches which lovingly serve communities that are suspicious of them reveal where their hope lies. They rouse the curiosity of those who reject their message yet benefit from the outworking of their hope.

Are you an urban church? Chances are, you are surrounded by people of vastly different social and economic settings, all trying to make a go of it in a lonely city. How can you serve them? Through English-language groups? Free financial advice? Child-minding facilities? A breakfast program at the local primary school? The possibilities are endless. God has made a habit of reaching people in cities. After all, his promised future is a city coming down to earth!

Or are you living in a battler area—a place of domestic violence and food shortages? A friend's church in my home city runs a food distribution centre—but it's more than "drive up and get a box of non-perishables". Time is taken with each client, tea and coffee are available, seating is ready. People who may have talked to no one all week, or have only been screamed at, are heard and spoken to in love. They are often open to hearing about Jesus. Creating a team to run this ministry is daunting, but God can provide. Chances are, you already have front-line servants, back-stage players, and those natural, pastorally caring evangelists who love telling hurt people about the Saviour.

Or perhaps, like so many, you live in the commuter belt. Your suburb empties out in the morning and refills in the evening. People are stretched for time with a complex network of commitments: family, work, leisure and all of the "have-to's" that leave little margin. What about serving the community at the weekend, assisting at local sports clubs, or signing up to the parents' committee at your children's school? What about asking the local council how your church can volunteer? What about being the church that just takes the pressure off those who are feeling pressured?

Whatever you do, leave your community that little bit better than the way you found it. Why? Because God has promised a new creation. We have the mandate to showcase that new creation now, in fractured but real ways, as we await its fulfilment. We can assess the brokenness of our location or investigate what pressures people in our area are likely to be under, and prayerfully respond to these things.

None of what I have written seems especially impressive on the surface. It won't look swish on a Prezi or a PowerPoint. It may not leave you with a healthy balance sheet financially. But I am convinced that a strategy that preferences God's people, proclaims God's praises, and promotes God's promises is the foundation for a church that is at risk of losing its nerve and leaving aside God's building project in a suspicious age. God is inviting us into a bigger and more satisfying building project than our panelled houses can offer us. Let's not spend all our energies renovating the wrong house.

Endnotes

[1] www.youtube.com/watch?v=PhhC_N6Bm_s (accessed 8 Oct. 2020).

7. When the Culture War Comes to You

(A Strategy for the Workplace)

So, you go into the office for work one day and everything has changed. Well, not *everything*. Your office chair is the same; your inbox contains the all too familiar to-do list it had on Friday; the coffee quality has not changed. Nonetheless, something is different. You can *feel* it. Then the directive comes down from Human Resources: the company's social policy is being recast to enable it—to enable *you*—to promote the LGBTQI community more positively.

A senior LGBTQI consultant has spent six months with your HR department, aligning this strategy with performance appraisals. Her charge? The company has been rewarding the wrong people. And that is going to change. Your next contract review will, in part, be determined by your promotion of the new equality and justice campaign.

It's also a financial campaign, since companies that refuse to positively promote equality are bound to lose out on the pink dollar. Social media pounces on inconsistencies. Cancel culture is real. Look at Chick-fil-A, Hobby Lobby and the Salvation Army, who all thought they were too big to be affected by this cultural shift—until they weren't. Ethical investors are asking hard questions before deciding where to put their money. This could be a big deal for your company.

You have long been a diligent and honourable employee in the political maelstrom of the office: a faithful witness to the gospel in word and deed. You want to see your office flourish and your company do well, and you especially want people to be drawn to Jesus! You've championed liberty and justice. But *this*?

Meanwhile on Sundays, your pastor exhorts you to be bold for Christ in the workplace. What is there to lose except your reputation? Your job, that's what! What could a pastor possibly know about life in the world out there on Monday morning? He is blissfully unaware of office culture—how hostile it can be to your faith and how suspicious of the Christian ethic it has become.

To top it off, the social club president is planning a Rainbow Day to launch the initiative. There'll be prizes for the most outlandish costume, followed by a special appearance by

Courtney Act, a local drag queen involved in the national campaign seeking equal pay for the nation's sex workers. The email suggests Friday week. As your floor's wellbeing representative, what can you do to help promote it?

The More Things Change...

If elements of that scenario are not familiar to you, they certainly will be to someone you know. But this kind of thing is actually nothing new. It's no worse—and certainly has less adverse consequences—than what Daniel, one of the Jews who was exiled to Babylon, experienced as an advisor to King Darius of Persia in the 6th century BC.

Daniel goes to work one day to discover that everything has changed—and it won't be his job on the line but his life. It's nothing to do with justice but with jealousy. His work colleagues look unfavourably at his success and at his intended promotion by the king. There is only one way to bring Daniel down:

> They could find no corruption in him, because he was trustworthy and neither corrupt nor negligent. Finally these men said, "We will never find any basis for charges against this man Daniel unless it has something to do with the law of his God." (Daniel 6 v 4-5)

Just as the "sexular" culture has placed many Christians in the corporate crosshairs, so the soon-to-be announced religious ethic of the Persian court placed Daniel in the crosshairs of a despot king:

These administrators and satraps went as a group to the king and said: "May King Darius live forever! The royal administrators, prefects, satraps, advisers and governors have all agreed that the king should issue an edict and enforce the decree that anyone who prays to any god or human being during the next thirty days, except to you, Your Majesty, shall be thrown into the lions' den. Now, Your Majesty, issue the decree and put it in writing so that it cannot be altered—in accordance with the law of the Medes and Persians, which cannot be repealed." So King Darius put the decree in writing. (Daniel 6 v 6-9)

Sneaky move. And smart. In one fell swoop they appeal to the king's vanity, and Daniel is hoist on his own petard. He may serve in the court of the Persian king, but they know the king that really matters to Daniel is God. Maybe they'd heard Daniel at prayer and marvelled at its exclusivity, or maybe they'd trawled God's law until they found something to work with. Whichever, they came to the king with a clear agenda: all prayer and requests were to be made through Darius alone for 30 days. Gotcha!

 It's that "gotcha" feeling that shrinks the distance between the Christian worker in 21st-century London, New York or Sydney, and Daniel in exile in Babylon in the 6th century BC. Both face a crunch moment. Both are *religious* crunch moments. True, one involves an obviously religious act (prayer towards the God of Israel and away from the false idol of an imperial cult), while the other (the push to promote a sexual ethic that is against God's command)

may seem less obviously religious. Yet, as we've seen, sexual identity *is* the new religion: the thing proclaimed as the locus of deep and lasting meaning, where the truly authentic life is experienced. Sex is the new imperial cult, and the leaders and influencers who promote this new faith look no more kindly on disobedience than a group of scheming Persian administrators.

And it's not just in the offices of the big multinationals. Christians are also pressed hard in other vocations. The well-known cake-shop cases (Ashers Baking Co. in the UK and Masterpiece Cakeshop in the US)—in which small-business owners were forced all the way to their respective Supreme Courts after refusing to design cakes supporting gay marriage—were only the start. Teachers are particularly challenged by pushes to promote sexual diversity in the classroom. Doctors and mental-health staff are instructed that affirmation is the only legitimate response to young people seeking gender transition.

How can we respond to these pressures? Daniel exhibited three distinct qualities that enabled him to honour God in a hostile workplace: he was faithful, faultless and fearless. That's a template for us as we face increasingly complex ethical situations in our own lives.

Kneeling Before the True King

Now when Daniel learned that the decree had been published, he went home to his upstairs room where the windows opened toward Jerusalem. Three times a day he got down on his knees and prayed, giving thanks to his God, just as he had done before. (Daniel 6 v 10)

Daniel's fidelity towards God was a reflex. The king's edict did not change that. Daniel could have reasoned that, since the king saw him as indispensable, he could pay lip service to the king's edict and pray to God inwardly. After all, how much godly kingdom work could be done if he wound up eaten by lions? Yet unfaithfulness leaks—just as an unfaithful husband often lies in other relationships in order to hide his adultery. Daniel knew he must be faithful in every area.

Daniel's faithfulness went deep and wide because he knew where his hope lay. It's significant that he opened his window towards Jerusalem, God's city, to pray.

Daniel was facing towards a heap of rubble and stones, a city that had suffered an inglorious defeat; while Babylon, where he served, was so magnificent that it even took away the breath of its own rulers (Daniel 4 v 30). And he prayed in full knowledge that he might be sprung by those plotting his downfall (6 v 11). Yet despite all this evidence that his hope was on the wrong side of history, Daniel was faithful—as he had always been.

We, too, need faithfulness locked away before any edict is announced. You cannot take out of the bank what you have not put in. So how might we ensure that we are ready for whatever comes our way?

If you're a church leader, then prepare your people for the week *they* will be having, not the week *you* will be having. The vast majority of their time is spent with work, study and family: places where ethical pressures arise. Have you created a preaching, discipleship and pastoral care strategy that will support and guide them when the office, shop or kitchen table becomes a hostile battleground? Can you point them to books, courses or conferences that will help? Do you pray regularly for and with them about these pressures? A crucial task of the modern pastor is to prepare people for life in Babylon, Monday to Saturday (and increasingly Sunday!).

What about if you're out in the trenches? It would be wise to have a "faithfulness check"—to regularly lift the hood or bonnet and see how things are going. How is your private life? Your prayer life? What do you watch, and what do you read? How do you respond to criticism? Have you determined how much influence work is going to have in your life? Have you locked away your justification, finding it in Jesus rather than in your job description, pay scale or career opportunities?

I cannot recommend highly enough committing to a small group of fellow disciples who can support and guide you as you navigate this increasingly hostile public life. Self-examination is one thing; examination by others, another thing altogether. Form a group of fellow Christian workers from your church, in which together you can explore the principles that you will abide by when the pressure comes. What can you bend on without compromise? Where is there give and take? What will you hold the line on? You need to discuss and establish boundaries before the situations turn up, so that your response is reflexive, not reactive.

This is as true in the casual "McJob" world as it is in the corridors of financial, political and cultural power. Imagine a diverse group from your church, comprising a business leader, a nursery nurse, a local politician and a retail store worker. People from vastly different settings with a common aim to help each other be faithful at work.

In Luke 16 v 10, Jesus tells us that whoever is faithful in small things will be faithful in big things. If the frantic pace of your family life, work life and social life has worn you down and hollowed you out; if you have let faithfulness slide in your relationships; if you have left behind love, forgiveness and purity as you step into the dog-eat-dog office; if your career has become your functional saviour—then you will not dare to be a Daniel. There's no sense in deciding that faithfulness will kick in when it really, really matters. Because it won't! Start out faithful. Let that be your trajectory, wherever life takes you.

Making Sure the Mud Won't Stick

Daniel's disobedience to the king in one area delivered him to the lions. But his total obedience saved him from them. When rescued, his first concern was not what the king thought of him, but what the King thought of him. Darius' opinion was secondary to God's:

May the king live forever! My God sent his angel, and he shut the mouths of the lions. They have not hurt me, because I was found innocent in his sight. Nor have I ever done any wrong before you, Your Majesty. (Daniel 6 v 21-22)

Daniel still honoured his boss by offering the ritual "May the king live forever", but made it clear that he was unscathed because *God* found him faultless. This same king, towards whom all prayer was to be directed for 30 days, could no more stop the lions eating Daniel than he could stop the foolish edict.

Darius recognised this—and was impressed.

I issue a decree that in every part of my kingdom people must fear and reverence the God of Daniel.

For he is the living God
and he endures forever;
his kingdom will not be destroyed,
his dominion will never end.
He rescues and he saves;
he performs signs and wonders
in the heavens and on the earth.
He has rescued Daniel
from the power of the lions. (Daniel 6 v 26-27)

Being faultless is powerful: not just in deficit mode but in surplus mode too—not just in what we won't do, but in what we choose to do. If, after refusing to be swayed on ethical matters, you are scorned, disciplined, demoted or even let go from your job, it must be in spite of the way you live, not because of it. We must cultivate exemplary, grace-filled and generous lives that challenge any allegation that our beliefs lead us to be mean-spirited, hostile and dangerous.

I once worked in the police department as a public servant. A fellow believer and I would drive to work together and pray that we'd be faultless in a place that, while created to find and prosecute faulty behaviour in others, exhibited plenty of its own. People knew we were Christians. They mocked it, especially the hard-as-nails officers. And there was gossip, anger, drunkenness, and adultery in that office as people under pressure let off steam. Then one day we got a taste of the "last day"! One of the loud, brassy party girls of the crowd, while someone was dissing their spouse, pointed to me and my friend and said loudly, "How come these two are the only ones who speak about their wives as if they love them?" Every mouth was silenced.

What might surplus-building, blessing-another obedience look like for us today, even as we run the risk of running up a deficit because of our "harmful" views on ethical and sexual matters?

For your church it may look like spending time and money supporting victims of the sexual tsunami instead of merely criticising the destruction. Helping victims of sexual violence, offering support and shelter to young pregnant women or volunteering at local rehab clinics or food-distribution centres could be a start. There are many ways a church can lean in to faultlessness. Why not sit down and map out with your church leaders how you can help those scorched by so-called progressive sexual values? You could even involve work colleagues in a social-justice campaign.

Recently a Christian family in my city made the news for being rejected as foster carers, due (publicly at least) to their espousal of conservative Christian sexual ethics. I wrote a blog critical of the foster agency's ruling. However, every year my church prepares hundreds of cooked meals for that same agency's foster parents. And after discovering that our local area has the highest foster-care needs in our state, several of our families went through the foster-care program and now have children in their care long-term. The agency has written to us to express their gratitude for all that we do.

Obedience is complex. What do we stand firm on? Where should we flex? Imagine you're a Christian owner of a bed-and-breakfast hotel. Should you refuse a room to a gay couple? As a business, you must comply with anti-discrimination legislation. Should we expect the world to hold to a standard that is not recognized outside the gospel community? Scripture tells us not to engage with any "brother or sister" who is sexually immoral or greedy but applies no ban to those of that description in the world

(1 Corinthians 5 v 9-11). And what about love? The gay community is convinced already that Christians hate them. Are we not called to love our enemies and to do good to those who persecute us? Yet isn't giving a gay couple a room an implicit endorsement of their sexual choices? And what impact might hosting them have on your children?

If you are facing indecision over what faultlessness looks like, remember you're not the first. We are so familiar with Daniel's story that the idea of a righteous Jew being the chief minister of a hostile pagan nation no longer shocks us. Was his dilemma less than ours? I think not.

The complexity extends to many workplaces. But let me encourage you. If you are the conflict-resolution woman in the office; if you are known to deflect the boss's praise to others; if you help colleagues when they're struggling with workloads; if you are slow to gossip and quick to point out people's strengths; if you constantly offer support (and perhaps prayer) to the troubled or grieving; if you share meals and conversation with everyone from janitor to manager, and are as quick to go out for a lunch with the gay couple from marketing as you are to nip off to the office prayer meeting—then when you fall into deficit over hard cultural matters, the "king" will be conflicted over whether to punish you, just as Darius was over Daniel.

Courage Under Fire

What is the secret to resisting the cultural push that paints us as the bad guys? Is it just treating it as a white-knuckle ride? Gritting our teeth and hoping it passes? These cannot be long-term strategies. Sooner or later we will run out of knuckles and teeth.

The key is to put our fear in the right place. Daniel wasn't "scared" of God, but God's opinion carried more weight for him than the king's opinions (or the lions' for that matter). This big view of God gave Daniel a proper view of humans. Not a *small* view of humans. A big view of God means we do not fear other people, but we do not despise them either. Humans become the right size—that is, the same size as us, with all the same sorts of fears, hopes and dreams we have. We come to our opponents as equals in God's eyes.

Which means we can answer difficult questions or angry responses to our Christian faith honestly and lovingly. What should you do when asked why your God or your beliefs don't celebrate homosexuality as good and healthy self-expression? Because God is big, you can answer fearlessly. But because humans are the right size, you can answer lovingly. We have the chance to show that humans were created to place their identity—to find meaning and significance—not in something as fickle and fleeting as sex but in God. And to show that sex is designed to point people towards God and his good design for humanity. Sticking to this message may make you a friend. It may make you an enemy. But fearlessness, in the context of faithfulness and faultlessness, will certainly make you intriguing. People will be unable to categorise you. And that's the way it should be.

So how do we keep God big and people the right size? First up, attend a church in which God's bigness is front and centre, and his salvation plan through Christ for all of creation is explained and celebrated. You'll know if that's the case in your church by how people are treated, especially the broken, the annoying, the plain weird, the single, the same-sex attracted. Are they projects to be involved with or family to belong to? Are these people seen as being "the same size" as the wealthy, impressive and good-looking?

That attitude will flow over into all of life. The gay-activist colleague and the anti-Christian fellow teacher are first and foremost made in the image of a big God. It may be that no answer you give about such matters, save fully agreeing with them, will make you anything but small in their eyes. But don't get in first. If they are to despise you it must be in spite of what the rest of your life looks like.

If you're feeling brave, take a risk and join the company diversity committee—to ensure all diversities, not just sexual ones, are honoured. Secular people who have little understanding of how conservative religious communities work often don't know what to do with non-Western religious minorities and end up patronising them. So secularism can only celebrate diversity down to a certain level. Deep religious differences—which Christians can cope with and indeed can interact with— are no-go areas for those who wish to sideline spirituality or lump all religions into one general basket for fear of offending one group or another. We can offer a level of diversity that takes the faith of others seriously in a way that secularists cannot.

Surround yourself with a support team that can talk through the wisdom of your decisions and responses. Help each other lean in to fearlessness and away from disdain. We all need the collective wisdom of those who have had similar conversations.

Most importantly, look to the One who was indeed thrown to the lions after making "the good confession" before the political and cultural powers (1 Timothy 6 v 13).

The truth is that, like Daniel, you may be thrown to the lions—cultural ones. You may lose your job, your influence, your status. You may even lose friends and the approval of your family, no matter how lovingly you explain yourself. Your honour and respect for your opponent may not be reciprocated.

Yet our final hope is that Jesus' resurrection has ushered in a new age. We have not received it fully yet, but the Spirit's down payment means we are guaranteed that scorn, disgrace and being sidelined are not the end.

Not long ago, a friend of mine questioned the progressive sexual public program being pushed at his workplace. A fairly senior public servant, he was forced to move departments in order to be able to continue working. His response has been to maintain love and respect for colleagues, all the while knowing that his vindication will one day come from

Jesus. And in spite of the long-term trouble and upheaval it caused, he was filled with joy. Daniel's strategy—faithful, faultless and fearless—really does work.

8. The City and the City

In his award-winning novel *The City & the City,* China Miéville sets a murder mystery in the fictional twin cities of Beszel and Ul Qoma.[1] Beszel comes across as a grimy Eastern European city circa 1970: think old cars, shabby houses, grey serge suits on the men, headscarves and drab dresses for the women. The buildings are run-down and there's a general tiredness to the place. Ul Qoma, on the other hand, is similar to modern-day London or Singapore, with colourful, expensive shops and ritzy skyscrapers. Inspector Borlú, from Beszel, is tasked with solving the murder of a young woman, and the case requires him to travel between both cities on a regular basis.

But here's the kicker. Both cities, Beszel and Ul Qoma, occupy the same location. Or, more to the point, they are intertwined. Streets of one run next to streets from the other. The government buildings of Beszel nestle next to those of Ul Qoma. Some locations are strictly Beszel, others solely Ul Qoma, while in mixed areas—known as "crosshatch"—lines are more blurred and residents from each city mingle. Well, mingle is too defined a word for it. Citizens from the two cities speak different languages, are trained to ignore ("unsee") citizens of the other city, and risk being pulled up for "Breach", a punishable crime, should they refuse to comply.

These are twin cities—even conjoined twin cities, that share vital organs. But they may as well reside on different continents. Travel between them requires a passport, security clearance, and language and culture training. Beszel has a national state religion, while Ul Qoma is decidedly secular. In an act of literary genius, Miéville has created one geographical location with two completely separate operating systems.

Citizens of Another Country

Welcome to life for the people of God living in the Western world today. It feels like we are living in a different city to the secular lives weaving around us. We occupy the same physical location but are worlds apart. We mingle with those whose view of history—where it is coming from and where it is going—diverges from ours. We live alongside citizens shaped by cultural ideas that are alien and often hostile to our own; people who use the same terminologies but mean different things by them.

And we feel insecure. We feel like the citizens of Beszel: slightly worn out, on the wrong side of history, and committed to old ways that won't cut it in the new world. Secular Ul Qoma offers glitz and glamour, the rainbow of expressive individualism, the excitement of pan-sexual freedom and the confidence of being on the right side of history. And we sit in our drab corner cafes and walk past our dated shop fronts, trying to "unsee" these enticements.

But it's even more confronting for us than for Beszel's citizens. We don't simply work in buildings next to Ul Qoma buildings; we share the *same* buildings. We don't work parallel jobs; we are involved in work teams and sit in work spaces alongside Ul Qoma citizens. We don't go home to eat or play or even share a bed with Beszel citizens only, but with those from Ul Qoma, too. We commit Breach every day.

To make matters worse, the shift to Ul Qoma citizenship seems far easier than the shift the other way. New Christians take time to loosen the cultural and emotional shackles of their former city. Meanwhile many longer-term Christians drift towards Ul Qoma desires and practices, despite their stated Beszel values. And many who leave the Christian faith seem to assimilate with ease into their new setting, speaking the new language in next to no time.

This drift away, coupled with our own desire to relieve the tension of our struggle, leaves us hankering for a middle ground. We long to have the benefits of belonging to God's city without the increasing cost of that identity in its hostile secular twin. This book has been about how to navigate that tension: how to live in proximity to that city yet hold to the values of another. How to live for God's kingdom in a culture that wants the benefits of the kingdom without the King.

The goal has been to ensure that we reorient our lives towards God—not only with conviction and purpose but with joy and hope as well. There is little to be said for an angry, despairing fist-shaking Christianity. There is even less to be said for a Christianity that creates a gated community, complete with barbed wire and hostile border guards and in constant fear of Breach. There must be a way to live as a citizen of a heavenly country (Philippians 3 v 20), without full withdrawal. What might it look like to negotiate this increasingly complex twin-city reality? Again we turn to Scripture to see that we are not the first to experience this tension. Which also means we do not have to come up with solutions on the fly.

A Tale of Two Corinths

Central to the gospel's understanding of history is the conviction that the resurrection of Jesus ushered in a promised new age, replacing the present evil age.

The concept of these two ages is developed in the Old Testament. The book of Isaiah finishes with the hope of a new heavens and a new earth (Isaiah 66 v 22). For Isaiah, the present age was the age of brokenness, injustice, sin and death. The promised new age would swallow up the old age. So Jesus came to an Israel that was holding on to a threefold hope: that God would judge the wicked and vindicate the righteous; that God would provide a new creation in which his people would live in safety and holiness; and that God would pour out his Spirit upon this new creation. And it happened! The giving of the Spirit in Acts 2 completed the triple promise. The cross was the act of judgment, the resurrection *was* the first act of a new creation, and Pentecost was the arrival of God's Spirit, poured out to renew his people. New age ushered in!

Yet the old age did not disappear. The cross has paid the price for sin and guaranteed a righteous verdict for God's people on the final day—yet sin still exists. Jesus' resurrection doesn't mean we won't die in this age. The Spirit is given, but as a down payment of a future payout. The old age is hanging around like an unwelcome guest at a party.

This age still affects us, even though we no longer belong to it. It affects us externally, in that the world (by which I mean the rebellious expression of the created order against its Creator) hates the rule of God and therefore is opposed to God's people. And it affects us internally, in that even though we are new-creation people, we still sin, and we cannot defy the ageing and dying process.

This two-age framework, and the tension it brings to Christians, sits behind Paul's thinking when he writes these words to the Corinthian church:

For the message of the cross is foolishness to those who are perishing, but to us who are being saved it is the power of God. For it is written: "I will destroy the wisdom of the wise; the intelligence of the intelligent I will frustrate." Where is the wise person? Where is the teacher of the law? Where is the philosopher of this age? Has not God made foolish the wisdom of the world? (1 Corinthians 1 v 18-20)

Paul is highlighting the tension that Christians in Corinth—and London, New York, Sydney, Washington, Chicago and Johannesburg—must grapple with: namely the overlap of two ages. Christians are citizens of a new city while remaining part of the old city. Corinthian Christians had to live as citizens of New Corinth in Old Corinth. London Christians must live as citizens of New London in Old London. New York Christians must live as citizens of New New York in Old New York!

The Temptation to Belong to Old Corinth

The temptation to identify primarily with the old city does not go away. When Paul asks, "Where is the philosopher of this age?" the answer might come back, "Living right next door". The wise person of the world? That may be your lovely secular neighbours waving you off to church on Sunday morning while they sit on the balcony drinking coffee and reading the paper. You think to yourself, "Why does their way of doing life look easier?"

And that teacher of the law? That could be the academic your wife works with who enjoys tenure and publishes fantastic peer-reviewed articles. She is promoted in the department while your wife struggles with her less-than-helpful PhD supervisor, who constantly criticises her thesis because it runs counter to the discipline's secular narrative. The old age still seems full of life—still very much in control of the direction of the culture and the course of history.

This has never been more true than now. Secularism's progress narrative does not recognize the two-age framework of history. The church is chided for being on the wrong side of history over sexuality matters, or over our conviction about the exclusivity of Jesus—making us feel as if we're stuck in drab, dreary Beszel. Glitzy Ul Qoma is the future, and we are being left behind.

The draw towards conforming intellectually or morally in order to belong is always there. Indeed, it's tempting to commit "Breach" when the dopamine hit for doing that is so enticing. And the Corinthian Christians had been enticed. That's why they overvalued eloquence and impressive speech. That's why they showed prejudice against the poor and favoured the rich. That is one reason why they did not take sexual immorality seriously.

The same is true today. The confidence of the secular prophets about the rapid decline of the church, or the insistence among many church leaders that the church will only grow once it signs up to modern ideas around sex and identity, both enervate us and entice us. When we cast a quick glance at the other city, it doesn't look like the cesspool of vice and destruction we were promised it would be. In fact, at first glance, it looks pretty good! No wonder many a first-year university student packs in their untested Christianity at the first sign of pushback on campus. There is great reward for rejecting the tension and crossing into Ul Qoma in this age.

But only in this age.

Confidence for Christian Corinthians

There is tension, but there is confidence also. Paul says that God has already made foolish the world's wisdom. The contest is over and the intelligence battle has finished. The cross settled it. Jesus was raised from the dead. It's game over. It may not feel like that to us, and it certainly does not feel like that to the world, but Paul asserts it: cross wisdom has made worldly wisdom foolish. One day the new city will swallow up the old city. We can have confidence that, as we live out the gospel life, it is aligning with God's future.

The old era, with its redundant intelligentsia and superseded philosophers, is on the wrong side of history, even as it utters its pronouncements, tweets its tweets and creates its scornful memes. Its humanities courses that lay the blame for society's ills at the feet of Christianity and its Netflix series that scorn our faith are the dying gasps of an old order.

This is astonishing. This is mind-blowing. This is life-changing. The Corinthian Christians were the future.

Yes, they were living among pagans who on the whole had better incomes, higher levels of education, richer job prospects, bigger houses, and more opportunities for social advancement (1 Corinthians 1 v 26-27). But the Corinthian church was on the right side of history because the cross had changed the course of history.

The Joy of Belonging to New Corinth

The *truth* of what I have just said is motivation enough to pursue gospel-centred living. But it is not only *true*; it is also *good*! Ul Qoma is a façade. A very shiny, elaborate façade, but a façade nonetheless. And a lot of work must be done to maintain it.

The post-Christian identity framework is flimsy. It is built upon presuppositions smuggled in from Christianity, including convictions about the inherent dignity of human life and the nature of good and evil, but it rejects the foundations of those presuppositions. This framework is, therefore, inherently unstable, constantly shifting to admit new, often contradictory realities. Cultural heroes become villains overnight as their tweets surface from ten years ago. Liberal newspaper editors are sacked for allowing alternative views to be voiced. Once-progressive authors are abused online for being transphobic. No one is safe.

If this age is passing away, the things it values are also passing away. They have nothing substantial underpinning them, so they are vulnerable to the latest social shifts. By contrast, the foundations of the gospel, built upon the promises of God, do not shift and change. They are stable and secure—intellectually, relationally and psychologically.

The claim that our core identity is found in our sexuality has created uncertainty, anxiety and loneliness. An identity grounded in Jesus is strong enough to carry the weight of our weakness, our sin, our pain and fears—indeed of both our sexual brokenness and hopes. Sexual identity is proving to be a poor substitute for grounding our identity in Jesus. That is a—*the*—good and true foundation.

The constant need to either grapple for power or present ourselves as victims is also a fragile framework. We should not buy into it. The idea that we are mere victims fails to address the reality that the church has often behaved poorly towards those it has either victimised or ignored. And while identity politics paints a binary picture of oppressor versus oppressed as the only two permissible categories, that is a dangerous road to go down. The ground constantly shifts. JK Rowling is a cultural hero in one decade and a villain in the next. The more complex biblical picture of human nature—the truth that we are both victim and perpetrator—makes more sense of who we are and how we behave.

Meanwhile, the authenticity narrative is also a blind alley. How authentic must I be? What must I pay in order to be that authentic? Why do the rules around authenticity keep changing? Who will pay the emotional, financial and relational price for me to discover the real me? Many a life, many a family, has been destroyed by a futile search for the authentic self. By contrast, the steady drip-drip of putting others first and dying to selfish desire will continue to create transparency and honesty within our Christian communities.

At its core, this authenticity search is self-focused and selfish. The Christian community, meanwhile, is called to identify not just as "persons" but as "a people". We gather as God's people, as citizens of another city, to serve others who are serving us, because together we are serving him. There's something rich and attractive about the gathering of God's people that no glamorous party can match. That is a sure foundation. And it brings a joy and certainty that we are clearly not seeing in the secular world.

The Call to Live in Both Cities

The differences between the old city and the new city are clear enough. We are called to a gospel ethic, not a secular one. But the tension remains: the two cities still occupy the same footprint. How do we live as citizens of New Corinth in Old Corinth?

In the current conversation around how Christians can navigate this hostility, some people talk about fighting the culture wars politically and legally to win back lost ground; others advocate retreating into a subculture sealed off from the world. The truth is somewhere in between. After all, the same Paul who wrote 1 Corinthians 1 also wrote 5 v 9-10:

I wrote to you in my letter not to associate with sexually immoral people—not at all meaning the people of this world who are immoral, or the greedy and swindlers, or idolaters. In that case you would have to leave this world.

Paul is not suggesting that the Corinthians set up an alternative Corinth out in the desert, safe from all the "grubby people". It's a call to live in both cities. The world is immoral, greedy, swindling and idolatrous. Paul's concern is that the church should not imitate this—he's not suggesting that they should simply shut their eyes to it altogether.

So we do not simply shrug our shoulders about something as critical as abortion and say, "Oh well, the world no longer holds our values!" Instead, we point out the unthinking "mix and match" in secularism's ethics. The inherent dignity of the body and a resistance to any view that someone can use another's body as they see fit are Christian ideas, and are not inconsistent with opposition to abortion, either scientifically or ethically.

Yet even as we argue this intellectually, we cannot expect the world to be consistent. We must rub shoulders with those who are committed to human rights but whose ideas around abortion are abhorrent—and who flatly refuse to see their inconsistency. We must share workspaces and homes with people whose understanding of sex leads them to act in ways contrary to God's word.

There is still enough common ethical ground to discuss these differences and highlight the inconsistencies while championing the protection of the victims of this age. But gospel ethics cannot ultimately be compelled of those who do not have God's Spirit.

The key is this: are we proclaiming the gospel message, and practising the gospel ethic it demands, among ourselves *first*? Now is the time to get our own city in order. If refugees from the culture wars and the "sexular age" realise that the way we deal with sin, or the way we practise forgiveness or look after the single mother, is completely different to the city they have known all their lives—and much more likely to lead to flourishing than anything from that city—they will clamour to escape and become citizens of the new city.

Not that we need to be perfect. Acknowledging our failures is one reason why we gather as the church: we proclaim the gospel of repentance and forgiveness to each other, committing ourselves to God again and making ourselves ready to go out into the world. Then we do it again the next week. Every church gathering is a mini-withdrawal from the world, in order to return to the world ready for a fresh attempt to live out the gospel ethic.

Meanwhile, trade associations will continue to squeeze Christian practitioners on their ethics, demanding sign-off in exchange for accreditation. City firms will demand more allegiance around secular values. Education systems will increasingly single out Christian students and employees. LGBTQI activists will seek legal recourse against small-business owners who refuse to cooperate. Family members will disown Christians for holding to Jesus' view of humanity.

We're at a critical juncture. We must future-proof ourselves. So creating alternative education systems which are not hostile to the gospel, for example, is a good idea. However, engagement with the culture should continue. If we are to establish alternative institutions and workplaces that operate around a Christian ethic, we must not do so just for ourselves. There are plenty of non-Christian neighbours and professionals who will also be worn out by the secular culture and seeking an alternative.

A day may come when many public roles and private jobs are no longer open to us; but let's stay engaged while we can. While our viewpoint and actions are still legal, let's be brave enough to express and enact them. And then when we can't, or we are driven out, let's encourage and support each other, seeking creative ways to flourish—ways that will give meaning and plausibility to our citizenship of a new city.

The key to living confidently—and joyously—in this society is knowing that King Jesus is in control of the journey. His victory over death and sin and Satan means we are secure. We do not know where the next cultural twist or economic and social turn will take us but Jesus does. The new age has been ushered in by the power of his resurrection, and the old age—Old Corinth and all of its allures—is the walking dead, even if it doesn't recognise it.

We finish with Abraham, whose confidence in God grew as he endured his own rollercoaster ride:

> By faith Abraham, when called to go to a place he would later receive as his inheritance, obeyed and went, even though he did not know where he was going. By faith he made his home in the promised land like a stranger in a foreign country ... For he was looking forward to the city with foundations, whose architect and builder is God. (Hebrews 11 v 8-10)

The New Corinth, the New New York, the New Jerusalem... Call it what you will. But God will bring us to that city—or, more to the point, bring that city to us. On that day, the age of hostility and suspicion towards the people of God will give way to the age of eternal celebration.

Endnotes

[1] *The City & The City* (Del Rey Books, 2009)

Afterword

Plot spoiler alert: after William Foster realises he's the bad guy in *Falling Down*, there's no happy ending.

What about for Christianity, and us as individual Christians, as bad guys in the 21st-century? How does it finish up for us?

On one level, it depends on how we each respond to being one of the bad guys. We could despair, give up, retreat into little holy huddles and try to stop listening to the world's (sometimes accurate) accusations. We could fall into raging denial, publicly posturing—and Facebooking or tweeting—that we're being misunderstood and maligned, fighting perceived fire with real fire, burning everything and everyone that we think stands against us. We could, of course, blend into the culture, compromising, softening the truths of the gospel, and going AWOL on biblical ethics when it counts in the public square.

These would all be unhappy endings. But they're not the only options. Despair is not the only option—is not even an option—for those who, like Daniel, have a hope in the new Jerusalem. Denial is not the starting point for a community which was birthed in repentance and in an acknowledgement of our own sin before our Almighty God. Blending in is unnecessary for those who know where to find true goodness and flourishing.

Instead, you can accept that, in this time and this place in history, we just might have to put up with being the bad guys. And that can drive you back into the community of God's people and to all of the richness that dwells there, thanks to the unity gifted to it by the Holy Spirit. You can refuse to allow the atomising nature of modern individualism to get its grip on you and pull you away from God's people. And you can go forward together to engage with the world bravely and courageously and with love and concern: to continue to be all that Jesus has called us to be even when all the world sees is a black hat coming in its direction, and humbly but resolutely to hold out a different story and a better way and a happier ending.

We worship a God who delights in reversing roles: lifting up the humble and bringing down the proud, filling the empty and sending the full away empty-handed. We look to the God who will one day welcome us with love and joy. We wait for the day when he will say to those whom the world said were the bad guys, "Well done, good and faithful servants".

That's a good ending.

Acknowledgements

Thanks to the leaders and congregations of Providence Church in Perth, Western Australia, who are faithfully committed to living for Jesus in increasingly complex times. Their love for God and for the people they live among, work alongside and enjoy this city with is a great gospel encouragement. Thanks to Rory Shiner, Nigel Gordon, Oliver Lindsell, Tim Adeney and Simon Bibby. The godly wisdom and counsel of this band of brothers has helped shape my thoughts over the years. And thanks to Katy Morgan, whose editorial skills polished a very rough diamond!

thegoodbook
COMPANY

BIBLICAL | RELEVANT | ACCESSIBLE

At The Good Book Company, we are dedicated to helping Christians and local churches grow. We believe that God's growth process always starts with hearing clearly what he has said to us through his timeless word—the Bible.

Ever since we opened our doors in 1991, we have been striving to produce Bible-based resources that bring glory to God. We have grown to become an international provider of user-friendly resources to the Christian community, with believers of all backgrounds and denominations using our books, Bible studies, devotionals, evangelistic resources, and DVD-based courses.

We want to equip ordinary Christians to live for Christ day by day, and churches to grow in their knowledge of God, their love for one another, and the effectiveness of their outreach.

Call us for a discussion of your needs or visit one of our local websites for more information on the resources and services we provide.

Your friends at The Good Book Company

thegoodbook.com | thegoodbook.co.uk
thegoodbook.com.au | thegoodbook.co.nz
thegoodbook.co.in